'Brilliant. The most authoritative, calm and comprehensive account of the most contentious issue in the Western world. There is no better guide than Sumption through the arguments to the reality.'
Trevor Phillips, columnist and presenter

'No one truly interested in this most contested area of public life can afford to miss *What Is Immigration Policy For?* Whenever I want to know what is really happening with migration – if I need to know the truth rather than the partisan outpourings of populists or the frightened formulations of politicians – Madeleine Sumption's work is where I head. If only everyone else did. If only they would all read this excellent book.'
David Aaronovitch, journalist and author

'No topic is hotter or more divisive than immigration. Thankfully, we have the coolest head in the business sharing her accumulated wisdom with us here.'
**Sir Anthony Seldon,
historian, author and educator**

'In an area where independence, reputation and scrupulously presented evidence are all, this is a hugely important book.'
David Neal, former Independent Chief Inspector of Borders and Immigration

'This clear and straightforward guide illuminates for everyone the treacherous political swamp of immigration policy.'
Charles Clarke, former Home Secretary

'If you read one book on migration policy, make it this one. Your reliable guide through one of the most difficult challenges facing our societies.'
Alan Manning, London School of Economics and Political Science

The status quo is broken. The world is grappling with a web of challenges that could threaten our very existence. If we believe in a better world, now is the time to question the purpose behind our actions and those taken in our name.

Enter the What Is It For? series – a bold exploration of the core elements shaping our world, from religion and free speech to animal rights and war. This series cuts through the noise to reveal the true impact of these topics, what they really do and why they matter.

Ditching the usual heated debates and polarizations, this series offers fresh, forward-thinking insights. Leading experts present groundbreaking ideas and point to ways forward for real change, urging us to envision a brighter future.

Each book dives into the history and function of its subject, uncovering its role in society and, crucially, how it can be better.

Series editor: George Miller

Visit **bristoluniversitypress.co.uk/what-is-it-for** to find out more about the series.

Available now

WHAT ARE ANIMAL RIGHTS FOR?
Steve Cooke

WHAT IS COUNTERTERRORISM FOR?
Leonie Jackson

WHAT IS CYBERSECURITY FOR?
Tim Stevens

WHAT IS DRUG POLICY FOR?
Julia Buxton

WHAT IS FIFA FOR?
Alan Tomlinson

WHAT IS HISTORY FOR?
Robert Gildea

WHAT IS HUMANISM FOR?
Richard Norman

WHAT IS IMMIGRATION POLICY FOR?
Madeleine Sumption

WHAT IS JOURNALISM FOR?
Jon Allsop

WHAT IS THE MONARCHY FOR?
Laura Clancy

WHAT ARE MUSEUMS FOR?
Jon Sleigh

WHAT ARE NUCLEAR WEAPONS FOR?
Patricia Shamai

WHAT ARE THE OLYMPICS FOR?
Jules Boykoff

WHAT IS PHILANTHROPY FOR?
Rhodri Davies

WHAT ARE PRISONS FOR?
Hindpal Singh Bhui

WHAT IS TRUTH FOR?
N.J. Enfield

WHAT IS VEGANISM FOR?
Catherine Oliver

WHAT IS WAR FOR?
Jack McDonald

WHAT IS THE WELFARE STATE FOR?
Paul Spicker

WHAT ARE ZOOS FOR?
Heather Browning and Walter Veit

Forthcoming

WHAT IS ANARCHISM FOR?
Nathan Jun

WHAT IS ANTHROPOLOGY FOR?
Kriti Kapila

WHAT ARE CONSPIRACY THEORIES FOR?
James Fitzgerald

WHAT IS FREE SPEECH FOR?
Gavan Titley

WHAT IS INTERNATIONAL DEVELOPMENT FOR?
Andrea Cornwall

WHAT ARE MARKETS FOR?
Phillip Roscoe

WHAT IS MUSIC FOR?
Fleur Brouwer

WHAT ARE THE POLICE FOR?
Ben Bradford

WHAT IS RELIGION FOR?
Malise Ruthven

WHAT IS RESILIENCE FOR?
Hamideh Mahdiani

WHAT IS SPACE EXPLORATION FOR?
Tony Milligan and Koji Tachibana

WHAT ARE STATUES FOR?
Milly Williamson

MADELEINE SUMPTION is Director of the Migration Observatory at the University of Oxford, which provides impartial analysis of migration in the UK. Since 2016, she has been a member of the Migration Advisory Committee, which advises the UK government on migration. She also chairs the National Statistician's advisory panel on migration statistics. Madeleine has a PhD in Public Policy from the University of Maastricht. In 2017, she received an MBE for services to social science.

WHAT IS IMMIGRATION POLICY FOR?

MADELEINE SUMPTION

First published in Great Britain in 2026 by

Bristol University Press
University of Bristol
1–9 Old Park Hill
Bristol
BS2 8BB
UK
t: +44 (0)117 374 6645
e: bup-info@bristol.ac.uk

Details of international sales and distribution partners are available at
bristoluniversitypress.co.uk

© Madeleine Sumption 2026

British Library Cataloguing in Publication Data
A catalogue record for this book is available from the British Library

ISBN 978-1-5292-3858-7 paperback
ISBN 978-1-5292-3859-4 ePub
ISBN 978-1-5292-3860-0 ePdf

The right of Madeleine Sumption to be identified as author of this work has been
asserted by her in accordance with the Copyright, Designs and Patents Act 1988.

All rights reserved: no part of this publication may be reproduced, stored in
a retrieval system, or transmitted in any form or by any means, electronic,
mechanical, photocopying, recording, or otherwise without the prior permission of
Bristol University Press.

Every reasonable effort has been made to obtain permission to reproduce
copyrighted material. If, however, anyone knows of an oversight, please contact
the publisher.

The statements and opinions contained within this publication are solely those of the
author and not of the University of Bristol or Bristol University Press. The University
of Bristol and Bristol University Press disclaim responsibility for any injury to
persons or property resulting from any material published in this publication.

Bristol University Press works to counter discrimination on grounds of gender,
race, disability, age and sexuality.

Cover design: Tom Appshaw

In Memory of Demetri

CONTENTS

List of Figures, Tables and Boxes		xiv
Acknowledgements		xvii
1.	**Introduction**	1
2.	**What Is Immigration Policy Trying to Achieve?**	18
3.	**Skilled Work Visas**	42
4.	**Low-Wage Work**	58
5.	**Family Migration**	73
6.	**Unauthorized Migration and Enforcement**	91
7.	**Refugees and Asylum Seekers**	112
8.	**Conclusion**	148
Notes		169
Further Reading		194
Index		196

LIST OF FIGURES, TABLES AND BOXES

Figures

1.1	Permanent-type migration in high-income countries, by category, 2018–2022. OECD, *International Migration Outlook 2024*	4
1.2	US inspectors examining eyes of immigrants, Ellis Island, New York Harbor. Underwood & Underwood, Publishers, c. 1913 (Library of Congress, public domain)	7
2.1	A Polish delicatessen in the UK. Photograph by Joanna Kozak, 2016. Reproduced with permission	25
2.2	Share of respondents saying they would not want to have immigrants as neighbours. M. Fernández-Reino and M. Cuibus, 'Migrants and Discrimination in the UK', Briefing, Migration Observatory, 2024	39
3.1	'I'd call that highly skilled.' Cartoon by Matt Pritchett, 28 June 2019. © Telegraph Media Group Holdings Limited 2025. Reproduced with permission	45
4.1	Mexican agricultural labourers topping sugar beets in 1943 near Stockton, California. Photograph by Marjory Collins, Library of	61

Congress Prints and Photographs Division Washington, DC

7.1 Pro-refugee protesters outside Balmain town hall where an Australian Labor Party caucus meeting was being held. Photograph by Hpeterswald via Wiki Commons, published under CC BY-SA 3.0 licence — 132

7.2 The US side of a border wall between the United States and Mexico in Douglas, Southeastern Arizona. Photograph from the Carol M. Highsmith Archive, Library of Congress — 135

7.3 Monthly US Southwest border patrol encounters, October 2016 to September 2025. US Customs and Border Control (CBP), https://www.cbp.gov/document/stats/nationwide-encounters — 140

Tables

1.1 Preferred destinations for potential migrants — 12

Boxes

1.1 What would open borders look like in practice? — 11
1.2 How much migration is there? — 14
1.3 Who makes immigration policy? — 17
2.1 Is migration from Muslim-majority countries different? — 28

2.2	Immigration versus border control	35
4.1	Tying workers to employers	63
4.2	Does demographic decline require low-wage migration?	66
4.3	Shortage occupation lists and the technocratic dream	70
5.1	Who is eligible for family visas?	77
5.2	Exceptional circumstances	82
6.1	Illegal? Irregular? Unauthorized? Undocumented?	94
6.2	Whose fault is it? Narratives about unauthorized migration	97
6.3	Deaths at the border	99
6.4	Human rights applications for legal status in the UK	108
7.1	Deciding who is a refugee	117
7.2	Does the asylum system favour the least vulnerable?	120
7.3	Are climate migrants refugees?	121
7.4	Australia's 'Pacific Solution'	130
7.5	The United States' experiment with large-scale safe routes	136
8.1	Is there a 'right' amount of migration?	149
8.2	Numerical limits on migration	153
8.3	Can policymakers compensate people who oppose high migration?	158
8.4	Can advocates persuade the public to change their minds?	163

ACKNOWLEDGEMENTS

I am immensely grateful to everyone who provided comments on chapter drafts or in some cases the whole book, including Bridget Anderson, Meghan Benton, Jacqui Broadhead, Katharine Charsley, Jeff Crisp, Susan Fratzke, Zoe Gardner, David Goodhart, Adam Hosein, Alex Kustov, Rob McNeil, Alp Mehmet, Sergi Pardos-Prado, Jonathan Portes, Martin Ruhs, Bernie Sumption, Jonathan Sumption, Sanne van Oosten, Peter Walsh, Stephen Webb and Paul Yates. Thanks to Meghan Benton and Natalia Banulescu-Bogdan for allowing me to hijack their summer holiday with brainstorming meetings. Huge thanks go to George Miller, whose many ideas and suggestions have greatly improved the book.

Had Demetri Papademetriou still been with us, I would have sought his counsel too. Nobody else taught me more about migration, and many of his ideas are in this book.

1
INTRODUCTION

At Ellis Island in New York Harbor in the early 20th century, doctors inspected prospective immigrants for signs of contagious diseases and other ailments before admitting them to the country. In many European countries today, rich non-citizens can get a residence permit in return for a business investment of a few hundred thousand euros. In Singapore, migrant domestic workers must show a negative pregnancy test every six months if they want to stay in the country. And in the United Kingdom (UK), people who want to obtain permanent residence or citizenship must pass a test to demonstrate their knowledge of everything from the Wars of the Roses to the film *Four Weddings and a Funeral*.

These are all examples of immigration policy. States use immigration policies to decide whom to admit and whom to exclude. These policies determine who can get visas to travel to a country, how long they can stay, what they can do during their stay, and what happens if they break the rules.

What is it all for? At the risk of stating the obvious, the purpose of immigration policies is to keep people out. Many people want or need to migrate, whether to join family members, work, study, or find somewhere safer to live. Governments and their electorates use immigration policies to separate 'us and them' – to decide who can join their societies and who cannot.[1] Politicians and the public often have strong views on what qualifies or disqualifies prospective migrants, from their skills and cultural background to family connections or need for protection.

Public debates about immigration are polarized. It has been one of the top issues for voters in high-income democracies over the past 20 years. Immigration was a major factor behind the rise of new right-wing parties in Europe, President Donald Trump twice winning power in the United States (US), and the UK's decision to leave the European Union (EU). Immigration is a major policy issue in its own right, and affects many other policy areas too – everything from the housing market and public finances to identity politics or the role of human rights law.

Governments face many dilemmas as they navigate these troubled waters. How should they balance economic and ethical goals? How much weight should governments give to the interests of prospective migrants versus the citizens who vote for them? How much hardship should governments put non-citizens through in the interests of enforcing immigration law? What are the limits of states' ethical obligations towards refugees? And once policymakers agree on the goals, can they actually achieve them with the policy tools at their disposal?

Migration comes in many different forms. When you think of a 'migrant', who do you have in mind? A 2023 poll asked respondents in the UK this surprisingly rarely posed question, and 65 percent singled out one of the smallest groups of migrants to the country: asylum seekers (that is, people who have applied to be recognized as refugees). Just over half thought about people migrating permanently, rather than temporarily.[2]

But migration comes in many other forms. International students, temporary workers, family members, retirees, and even wealthy people moving for leisure or to give their children a globally recognized education. Some move on visas and some get free movement rights as part of the EU or other international blocs. Some people settle permanently and become citizens. Others migrate for a few months or a few years. Some move repeatedly for seasonal work. Immigration policies are different for each of these groups. So are the dilemmas policymakers face – as this book will explore.

Figure 1.1: Permanent-type migration in high-income countries, by category, 2018–2022

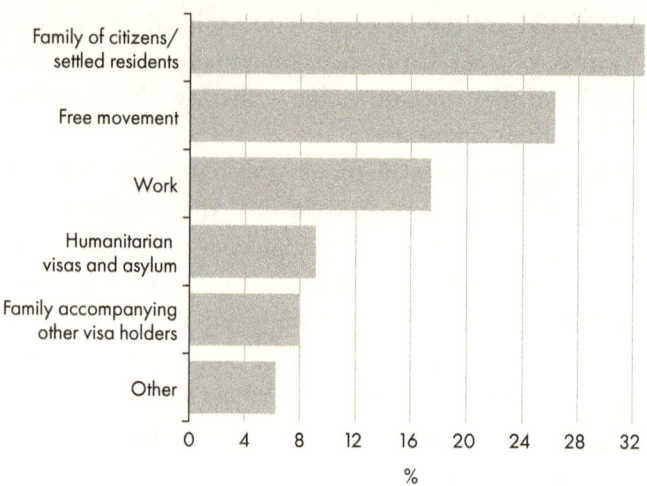

Note: Data covers the 29 high-income countries participating in the Organisation for Economic Co-operation and Development (OECD) for which standardized data is available. For some countries, data on family accompanying other visa holders are classified in other categories (for example, work or family of settled residents) and are likely to understate the true figure.

How did we get here?

Immigration policies in high-income countries today are extensive and detailed, with long lists of requirements for each type of residence permit. This is relatively new historically. Before the late 19th century, there was no system of continuous immigration control in Europe or North America. If you go back far enough, the concept of nation states with clearly defined borders did not exist in the same way as it does today. Borders were largely open.

Temporary restrictions were sometimes imposed during wartime to exclude suspected spies. For example, as refugees started to leave revolutionary France in 1792, an Undersecretary at the British Foreign Office wrote to his political master: 'By what I can learn, the majority of these people are of a suspicious description, and very likely either to do mischief of their own accord, or to be fit tools of those who may be desirous of creating confusion.'[3] The next year Parliament passed the Aliens Act 1793, which set up mandatory registration of foreigners – a measure that remained in place until 1836.[4]

Before the industrial revolution, there was a much bigger impediment to migration than immigration policy: travel was difficult and expensive, and knowledge of other climes limited. For most people, economic and social life took place in a small local area. Only the richest had the means or connections to travel more than a few miles.[5] Conflicts such as the wars of religion in Europe did sometimes drive people to move. Others were trafficked: enslaved Africans were being transported across the Atlantic as early as the 1480s.[6] But the cost and difficulty of travel prevented much voluntary migration.

The industrial revolution transformed migration by making long-distance travel and communication more affordable. It created new pushes and pulls. Population growth, revolutions and disasters such as the Irish potato famine in the mid-19th century pushed many more people to migrate – with large-scale movement both within Europe and from Europe to North

America. European traders, administrators, military personnel and missionaries migrated across the globe as colonial empires expanded in the 19th century.

Something resembling border controls started to emerge in the late 19th and early 20th centuries in response to this movement. Initially, immigration policies provided very little detail. For example, the US introduced entry restrictions in the 1880s. They included the infamous Chinese Exclusion Act targeting Chinese migrants, and restrictions on polygamists and people with 'loathsome or contagious diseases'. Beyond these exclusions based on very broad racial, physiological or moral grounds, immigration policies made no attempt to fine-tune who should be admitted. In the UK, the 1905 Aliens Act established the country's systematic border controls, requiring immigration officers to exclude 'undesirable immigrants'. This included anyone who 'is a lunatic or an idiot', among other characteristics.[7]

In the early days, there was nothing like today's detailed rules and guidance, with thousands of pages setting out everything from what counts as a 'shortage occupation' to how much paid work international students can do and how to tell whether a family relationship is genuine. After all, government bureaucracies were less centralized and had limited capacity. They would have struggled to administer complex public policies even if they had wanted to.

Even today, not all countries have formal immigration policies like these. The process for applying to live or

INTRODUCTION

Figure 1.2: US inspectors examining eyes of immigrants, Ellis Island, New York Harbor

An eye witness at Ellis Island reflected on the experience of immigration control in its early days:

> The immigrant, in his first moments at Ellis Island, is a bundle of emotions – timidity, surprise, fear, and expectation. These feelings are a testament to the enormity of the journey he has undertaken.
>
> It is a busy island. Yet in all the rushing hurry and seeming confusion of a full day, in all the babel of language, the excitement and fright and wonder of the thousands of newly landed, and in all the manifold and endless details that make up the immigration plant, there is system, silent, watchful, swift, efficient.
> (Extract from Dr Alfred C. Reed, US Public Health Service, Ellis Island)

work in many developing countries is less well defined. It may involve a lot of discretion, and many people move without formal permission. This book focuses the ideas behind formal immigration rules, and does so in high-income countries where such rules are most likely to exist and have been elaborated in most detail.

Before we get to those ideas, let us take a brief detour to consider why we have immigration policies at all – and the ethical questions behind them.

Is immigration policy justifiable?

Beyond the political debate, moral philosophers disagree on whether excluding foreigners is ethically justifiable. Migrants themselves stand to benefit enormously from migration. Moving voluntarily across borders allows some people to earn vastly more and enjoy a higher standard of living than they would at home, for example. It allows others to live with their loved ones, or escape from danger.

Immigration policies restrict this movement. As a result, the moral debate focuses on whether states can justify prioritizing the preferences of existing citizens who want to limit migration over the interests of people who want to move.

Open borders

Some argue that the only morally defensible position is to allow people to move for almost any reason – a position known as 'open borders'. The main basis for this position is that human beings are morally equal regardless of where they were born, and so have the same claim to live in the country they wish.[8]

Critics of immigration restrictions argue that they perpetuate global economic and racial inequalities by preventing poorer people and people of colour from moving to wealthier societies to improve their prospects or safety. Some also propose that states (such as the US and the UK) have a responsibility towards people from countries where war or colonial rule contributed to instability (such as Vietnam in the 1970s and 1980s, or Iraq after 2003).[9]

Other arguments focus on the practical consequences of migration control, which are often implemented using physical force – in what one academic calls a 'militarized form of global apartheid'.[10] Yet others take a more utilitarian perspective, saying that because migration from low- to high-income countries dramatically increases a person's productivity, freer migration is an efficient way to increase global gross domestic product.[11]

The main ethical defence of immigration controls is that states and citizens have the right to prioritize existing members of the community over prospective migrants. Citizens or their governments might want to restrict growth in the population of people sharing scarce resources such as land, or they might want to reduce the pace of change to social norms and culture that they feel have contributed to making their country successful.[12]

Philosopher David Miller makes an analogy with the family, arguing that it is widely considered morally acceptable to love your family more than someone down the street, and to share resources with family that you would not give away to others – even if those others are sometimes in serious need. If we are allowed to prioritize family over non-family, he argues, a state should similarly be able to prioritize its own citizens over prospective migrants.

A related defence of immigration policies is that open borders are incompatible with democracy in the current world order, unless there is a dramatic change in public opinion in high-income countries. One cross-country survey found that no more than 10 percent of citizens agreed the government should 'let anyone come who wants to', in most of the 17 countries with comparable data.[13] Miller also suggests that restrictions enable governments to offer more rights to those who *are* admitted, because there would be less demand to ration access to welfare, housing or other public benefits to newcomers.

Interestingly, some autocracies have used freedom from the constraints of public opinion to pursue more liberal or racially egalitarian immigration policies – such Libya's openness to large-scale migration from sub-Saharan Africa in the 1990s and 2000s.[14] Elected governments in high-income nation states today are more constrained by public opinion, which generally supports having at least moderately restrictive immigration policies.

Box 1.1: What would open borders look like in practice?

A poll of around 450,000 adults in 152 countries, conducted between 2015 and 2017, estimated that around 750 million people – or 15 percent of the world's population – would like to migrate to another country if they could. Of course, talk is cheap. Not all would actually move if there were no immigration restrictions. Many would lack the resources. Others would change their minds. But the data do show that the *potential* demand to move is high, particularly to the most popular destinations.

Among people who wanted to migrate, the largest number – 158 million – wanted to move to the United States (US), equivalent to just under half the US population. The number of people who wanted to move to Canada (47 million) exceeded the entire Canadian population.

It is difficult to predict precisely what would happen if high-income countries removed most or all of their immigration restrictions because it has not happened in recent history. But it is reasonable to assume the impacts would be profound.

In the United Arab Emirates, which greatly restricts migrants' rights but has very liberal entry policies, migrants now make up more than 80 percent of the population. Migration has been central to the country's economic success and citizens have become wealthy on the back of this (rather exploitative) model. Nobody would deny that migration has changed society there beyond recognition.

Table 1.1: Preferred destinations for potential migrants

Destination	Percentage (2015–2017)	Estimated number of potential adult migrants (millions)	Total population, 2023 (millions)
United States	21	158	335
Canada	6	47	40
Germany	6	42	83
France	5	36	68
Australia	5	36	27
United Kingdom	4	34	68
Saudi Arabia	3	24	33
Spain	3	21	48
Japan	2	17	125
Italy	2	15	59

Source: Gallup World Poll 2015–2017, https://news.gallup.com/poll/245255/750-million-worldwide-migrate.aspx. Population data: https://data.worldbank.org/indicator/SP.POP.TOTL.

A much more limited experiment with open borders has taken place in the EU, which gives all its citizens free movement within EU Member States. There is no comparison with open borders to the whole world, however: while there are some significant income differences between EU countries, they are not very big by global standards.

One thing the EU experience does tell us is that liberal immigration policies can be met very differently by publics in different places. A backlash against free movement in the UK was a major factor behind the 2016 'Brexit' vote to leave the

EU. The UK had been one of the most popular destinations for EU citizens, perhaps because of its welcoming labour market and probably also because when several new Eastern European states joined the EU in 2004, it did not impose initial restrictions on free movement like most other Western and Southern European countries did. After 2004, the UK's EU-born population increased by more a million within a few years, and more than two million over a period of 15 years – equivalent to about 3 or 4 percent of the population.[15]

But other EU countries, such as Austria and Ireland, also had substantial EU migration. It did generate political controversy,[16] but the backlash was smaller. One explanation is that their citizens had a much stronger feeling of European identity.[17] Citizens appear more willing to accept high levels of migration when they perceive the people who move to be culturally similar to them – a point we'll come back to in the next chapter.

Closed borders

At the other end of the spectrum, some people argue that their government should stop *all* immigration. As the rest of this book unfolds it will become clear why this position would not be possible to maintain in any country that wanted to remain a high-income democracy.

Almost every country allows people to travel in and out for short-term trips such as tourism or business. Unless the government completely prevented travel for

Box 1.2: How much migration is there?

An estimated 280 million people worldwide lived outside their country of birth in 2020 – around 3.5 percent of the global population.[18] In absolute terms, migration within low- and middle-income regions – for example, within Asia or Africa – has outpaced migration from the poorer to wealthier regions like Europe and North America in the first quarter of the 21st century.[19] Nonetheless, international migrants make up a much higher share of the population in high-income countries than in lower-income ones, because their populations are smaller.

In most high-income countries, roughly 10 to 20 percent of the population was born abroad by the mid-2020s, including people who migrated and then became citizens. There are outliers, however. The United Arab Emirates had close to 90 percent, while Japan had only around 2 percent foreign born – in both cases the result of quite different immigration policy choices.

The main countries of origin for migration vary greatly between high-income countries. In the UK the top country of birth is India; it is Algeria and Morocco for France; and Colombia and Venezuela for Spain. Migrants' decisions are influenced by economics, geography, former colonial ties and shared language. The British-Sri Lankan novelist and racial justice campaigner, Ambalavaner Sivanandan, famously said: '[W]e are here because you were there.'[20]

its own citizens and eliminated any domestic tourism industry – North Korea style – citizens would inevitably form families with prospective migrants and demand visas for family unification. If there was no option to get a visa, some people would still move without permission for family, refuge or work.

Most industries could broadly survive without migrant workers, though some are utterly dependent on it – such as seasonal horticulture. Global trade and foreign direct investment would be very difficult if it was not possible for executives and specialists to migrate at least temporarily to oversee business. Cultural exchange with other countries would be very limited, and it would be difficult to form dynamic global hubs for tech, science or the arts – all of which tend to draw on international staff.

The open and closed borders positions are philosophically interesting, but ultimately straw men. In practice, most high-income countries have policies that permit substantial migration – enough to see the foreign-born share of the population rise year after year. But they also prevent many – probably most – people who would like to move from doing so.

My perspective

Immigration does not align neatly with left–right divides. A more meaningful dichotomy is between people with liberal versus sceptical views on migration. You don't have to identify as either. As I'll discuss in the final chapter, intellectually coherent policy positions exist that combine liberal and restrictive preferences on different types of migration, such as economic versus family or humanitarian.

Experts and commentators on all sides of the debate present the answers as obvious – if only governments had the 'political will' to follow their guidance. Many also demonize their opponents. Pro-migration liberals often see people with sceptical views as heartless racists who don't care if migrants suffer. Sceptics often see liberals as moral bullies who stifle legitimate debate about real impacts of migration that a large share of the population cares deeply about.

I do not think the answers are obvious. Almost all changes to immigration policies have winners and losers. This is because immigration policymakers juggle conflicting goals, such as economics, social cohesion and fairness towards both migrants and citizens. Deciding which policies are most ethical is particularly difficult: and as human beings we tend to be overconfident in our ability to determine what is morally right.[21]

The problems continue once we get to the nuts and bolts of implementation. Immigration policies often just don't work very well. Incoherent or apparently contradictory policies often arise from the basic reality that governments cannot achieve everything they would like at once.

This book will not try to convince you to support a particular set of policies. Instead, it will provide the evidence to help you decide for yourself. If you already have a view on what sort of migration policy you want, perhaps it will even convince you to see some of the arguments from the other side.

Many experts criticize how policymakers manage migration. Surveys often find that trust in governments' competence on migration is low. Many of the critiques are valid. For example, we will see plenty of cases where politicians are not honest about the trade-offs, or say one thing and do another. But if I do my job well, you might even start to feel some sympathy for immigration policymakers. Sometimes policies go wrong and it's not because politicians lacked the wit or will to do the right thing. They just have a really difficult job.

> **Box 1.3: Who makes immigration policy?**
>
> This book uses the term 'immigration policymakers' to talk about everyone who is involved in decisions about immigration policy. In most high-income democracies, responsibility is shared between elected politicians (who pass laws) and government departments, ministries or agencies (which define the policies in more detail and then implement them). The government agencies are typically run by either elected politicians or political appointees, and staffed by civil servants. Government structures vary, so a policy decision that would be signed off by the head of a government department in one country might be written into legislation in another. 'Immigration policymakers' is thus a catch-all term to refer to them all.

2
WHAT IS IMMIGRATION POLICY TRYING TO ACHIEVE?

Imagine you are an immigration minister deciding how many refugees to resettle from a conflict zone. The media is focused on the conflict and people are asking why the country isn't 'doing its bit'. Refugees would benefit enormously from a safe route to rebuild their lives. However, your civil servants tell you that each refugee will need a lot of financial support over their lifetime, and public finances are already extremely tight. You told voters you were going to reduce migration, not increase it. And it's not clear where newcomers will live, as there are already housing shortages. Voters seem to think resettling more refugees is the right thing to do *now*, but their attention will move on with the media cycle. Do you welcome more refugees for ethical and short-term political reasons? Or do you prioritize medium-term economic goals instead? If you decide to admit more refugees, how many and which ones?

Next in your in-tray is a petition from employers in the childcare sector asking for a special work visa for nursery workers. They say they're already doing all they can to attract local workers and can't increase wages without hiking the prices they charge. More affordable childcare would help working families. But job-specific work visas in low-wage jobs are riddled with problems. You're already dealing with some pretty nasty cases of exploitation among seasonal agricultural workers. And what if employers lose the motivation to look for local staff once they can easily recruit from overseas? Maybe the solution is to forget about a visa programme and subsidize the childcare sector more heavily instead – but your colleagues in the finance ministry aren't keen to pay up.

Immigration policymakers are constantly faced with trade-offs like these. All the options have winners and losers, and policymakers have to decide which goals to prioritize. Even then, it is often unclear which policies will work and which won't.

Later chapters will look at how governments address these dilemmas in the main areas of migration policy: work, family, asylum and unauthorized migration. But first, this chapter considers some of the goals that surface repeatedly: economics, social cohesion, security and ethics. This list is not comprehensive. Foreign policy often plays a role, for example: requests for visas frequently crop up in trade negotiations. But the four points that follow cover the most salient questions.

Economics

Look through the op-eds and you will get the impression that our future prosperity hinges on how we handle immigration. 'Immigration is destroying the economy', reads one. 'Without immigrants, our economy would be a disaster', reads another.

The reality is less exciting. Immigration is not the solution to all our economic problems and it is not the sole cause. Migration has economic positives and negatives. Both the benefits and costs are often smaller than people imagine.

Research on how immigration in Europe and North America in the 1990s and 2000s affected wages has found evidence of negative impacts on low-wage workers and positive ones on the highly paid. Negative impacts on lower-paid workers appear to be less likely when the economy is healthy and dissipate within a few years.[1] Nonetheless, the impacts in most studies are surprisingly small.[2] A typical study found that each year from 1994 to 2016, migration to the UK had reduced the wages of the lowest earners by around half a penny per hour.[3]

The impacts of migration are genuinely difficult to measure, and it's likely that existing studies have struggled to pick up some impacts. It's also likely that immigration policy simply isn't a powerful tool for helping local workers. While migration increases the number of workers competing for jobs, it also increases the number of jobs: employers make use of the workers available to them and expand production. This may explain why immigration seems to have limited impacts on both wages and employment rates. In the medium term, the main impact is to increase the population, and countries with larger populations will not necessarily be richer or poorer than less populous ones.[4]

Immigration matters a lot to certain employers, but this does not mean it is crucial to the economy or population as a whole. For example, farmers growing soft fruit and other seasonal produce rely heavily on migrant workers. Without seasonal workers, many would cease to operate. The country would import food instead. Policymakers might want to support farming for non-economic reasons, such as to boost food security or slow the decline of rural communities. However, horticulture makes up a tiny share of the overall economy in all high-income countries. From a purely economic perspective, how many strawberries the economy produces does not matter very much. The same applies to many other low-wage intensive industries.

Nonetheless, some of the economic impacts are meaningful enough that they cannot be ignored. First, immigration contributes to higher housing costs in places where house-building does not keep up with population growth, like the UK, US or Australia. The empirical evidence on the size of this impact is still patchy, but the theory is convincing.

Second, immigration is likely to affect productivity – a measure of how much the economy can produce from given amount of inputs such as people, land or machinery. In the long run, productivity is incredibly important to living standards. The impact of immigration on productivity is disputed, however. In theory, we might expect highly skilled migration to increase productivity, especially if newcomers are involved in innovation or R&D – for example, scientists inventing new technologies. We might expect migration into less skilled, labour-intensive roles to reduce average productivity if employers no longer have such a strong incentive to adopt labour-saving technologies such as robotics in warehouses. That said, even migration into low-skilled jobs might in theory positively affect non-migrants' productivity if it enables locals to move up into more skilled jobs. There is evidence for all these effects.[5] Looking at the aggregate impact of migration on productivity, several studies find large positive effects,[6] although some find close to none.[7] The jury is still out on this issue.

Finally, the economic impacts of migration are sometimes small on average simply because positives and negatives happen to cancel out. Take the impact on public finances – that is, whether migrants pay more in taxes than it costs to provide them with public services or benefits. One analysis from the UK's official budget forecaster looked at this 'net fiscal impact' over the course of migrants' lifetimes. It found that a representative high-wage migrant who lived until age 85 would bring a net benefit of over £900,000 to public finances, while a representative low-wage migrant would cost more than £750,000.[8] These impacts may roughly cancel out today, but that won't necessarily be true forever – it depends on policy decisions towards different types of migration.

Not all migration is the same. And for many of the economic impacts, *who* is migrating is more important than how many. The evidence still has many gaps, but it seems likely that the economic benefits of migration come primarily from migration into highly skilled jobs.

Society and culture

> We need not be afraid that these new influences will somehow threaten the 'British way of life': on the contrary, a new resilience derived from diversity can only strengthen Britain. (UK Prime Minister Margaret Thatcher, 1985)[9]

> Immigrants have a major responsibility for their integration into Danish society. They must learn Danish, and they must accept the fundamental values on which our society is based. We must make it clear that in Danish society men and women have equal rights, that we do not accept forced marriages, and that we refuse to accept that oppressive family patterns can be explained and excused by references to differences in culture and traditions. (Danish Prime Minister Anders Rasmussen, 2003)[10]

Policy debates often focus on economics, but research suggests that people's attitudes towards migration depend even more on their feelings about its social and cultural impacts.[11] One UK study found that while people cared a lot about immigration policy's economic benefits, many were willing to sacrifice personal income in return for lower levels of migration.[12]

Analysing the social and cultural effects of migration is hard because people disagree on what a 'good' outcome looks like. Survey respondents in Europe are divided on whether immigration has positive or negative effects on cultural life and whether it makes their country a 'better place to live'.[13]

One measure of social resilience that most people agree is important is trust. American political scientist Robert Putnam famously argued that ethnic diversity reduces trust in the short run. A wide range of studies confirm his findings, although others dispute them.[14] The reasons diversity might reduce trust are debated, but it appears that people are less sociable when their neighbours are more different from them. People are also more willing to make sacrifices for the common good when they empathize or feel similar to the people who will benefit.[15] However, cultural diversity may also have benefits. Some studies suggest that it makes teams of people more creative or more likely to come up with new inventions, for example – although these results are similarly disputed and may be more relevant to the professional classes than the majority of the population.[16]

Debates about positive or negative social impacts usually hinge on the idea that migrants differ from the imagined 'us' that makes up society. This is both true and problematic, for several reasons.

First, attitudes, values and behaviour vary enormously within both migrant and non-migrant populations. There is no single 'we' or 'they'. Traits ranging from religious beliefs and childbearing choices to whether

Figure 2.1: A Polish delicatessen in the UK

After Poland became a member of the European Union (EU) in 2004, Polish retailers became a feature of many British towns and cities, serving a growing Polish migrant community

people smoke vary widely by country of origin.[17] There are also big differences between people from the same country of origin.[18] Within the local-born population, attitudes and behaviour depend on many factors too, such as class, education, age and geographical location. Statistics conceal this variation. They produce positive and negative generalizations that will be true of some people but not others.

For example, a negative stereotype is that some migrants do not accept same-sex relationships or egalitarian gender norms when they come from countries with more traditional attitudes.[19] A study of 32 European destination countries did in fact find that migrants from countries with traditional gender norms were more likely than non-migrants to agree with the statement 'When jobs are scarce, men should have more right to a job than women'.[20] Results varied widely by country of origin, with more conservative gender attitudes among people from the Middle East and North Africa than Latin America. However, most respondents did *not* agree with the statement, and they became less likely to agree with it the longer they had lived in their European home.

The same applies to positive stereotypes, such as the notion that migrants are unusually hard-working and aspirational. Again, we can find some evidence for this *on average*. One study found that recently arrived Eastern European migrants in the UK were less likely to take sick days from work, for example.[21] There is also evidence that migrants tend to have higher aspirations for their children.[22] Indeed, high migration is one of the reasons that scholars cite for the improved performance of London's schools after the turn of the millennium.[23] But of course there will also be plenty of children of migrants who do not do well in school. The data are only averages. Policymakers will thus go quite wrong if they assume that everyone conforms to the stereotype, whether positive or negative.

Second, social and cultural generalizations can easily be oversimplified to suit a given agenda. For example, people who voice concerns about migrants being homophobic or failing to support women's rights are not always particularly liberal on these rights themselves.[24] Generalizations also ignore important context. For example, migration liberals sometimes characterize migrants' rates of self-employment or their willingness to do 'jobs locals won't do' as signs of entrepreneurial spirit or dedication – though the reality is that people often take up these types of work because they have limited other options, and not because of any special moral virtue.

Third, the social impacts of migration are different in the short and long run. Newcomers adapt to their new societies over time and societies adapt to them.

On one hand, migrants tend to become more similar to non-migrants over time and across generations. For example, differences in attitudes towards gender and sexuality narrow or disappear for many migrant groups by the second generation (that is, local-born children of migrants).[25] But the patterns are not uniform and vary by country of origin (see Box 2.1).

On the other hand, destination societies also become more relaxed about newcomers' presence over time.[26] Differences that once seemed significant become less salient, such as the presence of visible minorities or people practising different religions. In many high-income countries, a level of ethnic diversity that was controversial in the 1960s became unremarkable by the 2020s. This matters because integration is not something that is done exclusively by migrants: whether migrants experience discrimination lies well beyond their control.

How should we interpret this adaptation? First, some commentators argue that concerns about social change due to migration are misplaced. One hundred years

Box 2.1: Is migration from Muslim-majority countries different?

The integration of Muslim migrants has been a controversial topic in many Western European countries. Muslim newcomers in Europe tend to fare worse than other migrant groups in the labour market,[27] are less likely to marry outside of their ethnic group,[28] and are more likely to have traditional attitudes prevalent in their countries of origin.[29] For example, one European study found that the gap in attitudes to same-sex relationships was larger for Muslims than for other migrant groups.[30] Similar to other migrant groups, local-born Muslim children of migrants were more liberal on the issue than their parents, although they remained less tolerant – on average – than people with no migration background.

In stark contrast, Muslim immigrants to the US from many of the same countries of origin have relatively good socio-economic outcomes. For example, Pakistani migrants in the US have considerably higher household incomes than the average American (although women do still have lower labour-force participation).[31] The majority hold a university degree and they are less likely to have poor language skills than other migrant groups.

So what explains the Muslim 'penalty' in Europe? A major factor is likely to be migrants' more disadvantaged backgrounds. The first cohorts of migrants from Muslim-majority countries to Europe arrived for work in low-wage industries such as textiles and had relatively few qualifications, while those heading for the US were more often highly skilled professionals.[32]

If Pakistani migrants' good economic outcomes in the US surprise European readers, US readers may equally be surprised that Mexican migrants on the other side of the Atlantic do rather well.*[33] One potential explanation in both cases is the size of the existing migrant community. Where existing communities are strong, it reduces the barriers to new migration, including for people with fewer resources. By contrast, Mexicans migrating to Europe will tend to be more affluent.

Some of the penalty Muslim migrants face in European labour markets also results from discrimination. For example, one study in France found that employers were much more likely to offer Senegalese job applicants an interview if they had a Christian- rather than Muslim-sounding name.[34] Culturally, there is also some evidence that people distance themselves from their European country of residence if they feel they are discriminated against or excluded.[35] While discrimination against Muslims also takes place in the US,[36] some scholars argue a more divisive public debate about Muslim migrants in Europe has created a particularly unwelcoming environment.[37]

---

* For example, while only 9 percent of Mexican migrants to the US held a university degree in 2023, the England and Wales Census showed that 75 percent of Mexican-born people in the England and Wales did, making them one of the UK's most highly educated migrant groups.

ago, Britons and Americans complained about Irish immigrants but now are perfectly happy with them. The same may be true for current migrants a generation or two from now. However, this minimizes the importance of people's experience now. People may dislike the changes they see around them, even if they are told that at some point after they are dead, their grandchildren won't understand what the fuss was about.

Second, if adaptation over time is important, it suggests that the scale and pace of change will make a difference: that is, how many people are added to the population and how different citizens (rightly or wrongly) perceive them to be. For example, some people may positively welcome a certain amount of migration, but worry about very rapid change.

In any case, immigration policies are not always very good at selecting people based on social or cultural impacts. Few policymakers want to ban whole nationalities from receiving visas for cultural reasons (although the Trump administration briefly attempted to do so in 2017, as I discuss later in this chapter). They can refuse people with criminal records (although getting accurate information on foreign convictions is not always straightforward). They can require newcomers to pass language tests. Both of these requirements are relatively common in high-income countries.

But selecting people based on their attitudes or values is both more controversial and less likely to be effective, since it is easier to lie about your beliefs than your diplomas. For example, the UK tries to test values through its official citizenship test, with questions such as:

> Which of the following statements is correct?
> A. There is no place in British society for extremism or intolerance
> B. Britain encourages people to have extreme views and act upon them.

Perhaps there is some value in ensuring that people know what they are *supposed* to say in answer to such questions. But we should not fool ourselves that policymakers can use civics tests to find out what people truly believe.

Another approach is to try to speed up the process of adaptation – for example, by helping newcomers learn the local language or find work that will bring them into contact with more non-migrants.[38] These are not simple tasks. They will usually cost money, just like any other programmes designed to improve people's skills or employment prospects.

Finally, policymakers concerned about social impacts can try to slow the pace of change by allowing lower levels of migration. They then have to decide which types of migration to restrict. This is not always easy, as will become clear over the course of this book.

Fairness

When the UK's Conservative government proposed in 2022 to prevent migrants and refugees who had entered the country illegally from claiming asylum, charities and opposition parties accused them of 'performative cruelty'.[39] They argued the policy was unfair on refugees, whom the UK had a moral duty to help regardless of how they had entered the country.

Prime Minister Rishi Sunak hit back with competing moral arguments, saying it was 'unfair that people come here illegally' from safe countries like France – for example, unfair on other refugees who might have greater need for asylum.[40] He claimed that cracking down on refugees entering illegally was the right thing to do because it would save lives by deterring others from risking dangerous journeys. In other words, both sides appealed to moral arguments in different ways.

People on either side of the debate agree that fairness matters. They often do not agree on what is fair or who we should prioritize being fair *to* – migrants themselves, or citizens of the destination country.

Australia and New Zealand periodically make headlines for denying visas to skilled work visa holders with disabled children on the basis that medical conditions impose costs on the state.[41] Some argue that this is unfair on people with disabled children – others that it would be unfair to make the Australian or Kiwi taxpayer pay the cost.

Another ethical dilemma is whether to give legal status to people who entered without permission or overstayed a visa. Some argue that unauthorized migrants should not benefit from bypassing the rules and that governments must have the right to enforce immigration law. Others believe that being deported is too harsh a consequence, particularly when migrants have built their lives in the destination country over many years and will be separated from family members. Fairness is in the eye of the beholder.

Moral debates such as these have an important place in immigration policy: policymakers face genuine ethical dilemmas. However, moral arguments are also divisive. They are often used to attack opponents rather than get to the bottom of difficult problems.[42] Politicians who agree on the goals but disagree on the precise methods of achieving them can have a pragmatic conversation and find the middle ground. People who think the opposition's perspectives are morally bankrupt have little scope for compromise.

In several areas of immigration policy, constitutional rights or human rights law adjudicates the conflict between states' rights to enforce their preferred set of laws and individuals' rights to avoid harsh treatment. This takes some decisions out of the hands of policymakers and into the courts. It effectively turns a political conversation about what is fair into a legal discussion about what is allowed. Experts have quite different views on whether this is a welcome development or not.

National security

'We're a nation of laws as well as a nation of immigrants', President Biden's departing Homeland Security chief Alejandro Mayorkas said in early 2025, stating that unauthorized migrants who 'pose a public safety threat' should be deported.[43]

National security crops up a lot in public and political debates about immigration. Some present migrants as villains, referring to 'invasions' or highlighting crimes or acts of terrorism committed by foreign nationals. Others present migrants as the victims suffering at the hands of ruthless people smugglers. Yet others see migration as a solution to threats – such as migrant seasonal workers boosting domestic food security.

In rare cases, discussions about security threats are central to debates about a particular immigration route. For example, debates about money laundering and financial crime have been central to the debate about investor visas, which admit very wealthy people whose source of funds is not always crystal clear. For the most part, national security concerns do not tend to play a large role in immigration policymakers' day-to-day discussions, however. There are various potential reasons.

First, foreign nationals who commit acts of terrorism or organized crime are not always migrants. Often, they are visitors. Immigration policy focuses on who can come to the country to live. However, the large majority of non-citizens who cross the border of a high-income country in any given year will be tourists or business visitors, not newly arriving migrants. For example, on 9/11 all but one of the 19 hijackers in the US had arrived on visitor visas rather than residence visas (one had a student visa).[44] Tougher rules on who can migrate or settle in the country would not have kept them out.

> **Box 2.2: Immigration versus border control**
>
> In the past, border control and immigration policy were more closely linked. Immigration policies were enforced primarily at the border. Once someone had gained entry, they could largely do what they wanted. This changed over the past 50 years or so, as many countries gained technological and administrative capacity to monitor people within their borders more closely. Consulates abroad vet prospective migrants before they issue visas to travel. And internal controls may require employers, police or others to check people's immigration status.

Second, because so few people commit crimes, identifying the people who have no criminal record but might commit crimes in future is like looking for a needle in a haystack. A controversial example of an attempt to do so was Donald Trump's executive order popularly known as the 'Muslim ban', which aimed to suspend immigration and refugees resettlement from seven Muslim-majority countries on the basis that they could have 'ties to terrorism' or hold 'violent ideologies'.[45] The ban was controversial because the policy tarred everyone with the same brush – including the majority who reject extremism and would never commit any offence.

Even if immigration policymakers struggle to identify 'bad actors' in advance, their policies may affect the risks of crime indirectly. For example, socio-economic disadvantage is a risk factor for both committing crimes or becoming a victim of crime.[46] Many immigration policies explicitly select people who have led relatively privileged lives, that is, people with high education and comfortable incomes. These policies probably also reduce the risk of admitting people with a higher propensity to commit crimes. Meanwhile, some economists have argued that immigration policies that exacerbate poverty by prohibiting or restricting work may increase the risk that migrants will become either perpetrators or victims of crime.[47]

Discrimination

Some analysts argue that the whole project of immigration policy is founded on racism, aiming to prevent people of colour from joining the community. Is this true?

Historically, the connection between racial discrimination and immigration policy is undeniable. Until the late 20th century, politicians in many Western countries openly discussed their desire to prevent non-White people from immigrating. For example, a programme officially known as the 'White Australia' policy in the first half of the 20th century relied on a literacy test that required migrants to write down 50 words dictated by a border official in a European language – much easier for Europeans than Asians. Almost all non-White migrants failed.

Racial prejudice has fallen considerably since then. In 1958, only 4 percent of US poll respondents said they approved of marriage between Black people and White people, but this had increased to 94 percent by 2021.[48] By 2020, only 3 percent of people in the UK agreed with the statement 'to be truly British you have to be White', down from 10 percent 14 years earlier.[49]

High-income countries' immigration policies no longer discriminate directly on race. That does not mean race has become irrelevant, however. Several recent studies put ordinary citizens in the shoes of immigration policymakers, asking them to prioritize between different profiles of migrants. A relatively consistent picture emerges.[50] Citizens in majority-White high-income countries tend to prefer migrants who are educated, employed and have language skills.* Women are more welcome than men. Doctors are particularly desirable. Citizens also often prefer non-Muslims and White migrants.[51]

One study in the UK – a country that tends to have relatively low measures of racial prejudice

---

* Poll respondents don't want to sound prejudiced, and would struggle to answer questions like 'Do you prefer non-Muslim migrants?' honestly. A rather clever study design gets around this problem by getting respondents to choose between a series of pairs of fictional migrants with randomly assigned traits such as religion, education or sex. Researchers can then see whether people consistently choose Christians over Muslims, even if respondents aren't aware that this is what they are doing.

by international standards[52] – found that survey respondents chose more restrictive policy options if they were told that higher migration would reduce the White British share of the population over the long term.[53] In other words, citizens discriminate on a range of factors, and race is one of them.

Do these preferences make their way indirectly into policy? It would be surprising if they didn't. It's difficult to prove in any specific case, though. That's because race is closely linked with other factors that also affect policy. Why did the UK open a large, uncapped visa scheme to welcome Ukrainians fleeing the Russian invasion in 2022, for example, but offer limited visas to Afghan refugees after the fall of Kabul in 2021, and none to Sudanese refugees after civil war broke out in 2023? Many critics pointed out that Ukrainian refugees were White. However, they also appeared sympathetic to the public for other reasons. Ukraine shared a 'common enemy' – Vladimir Putin – in a conflict British people largely understood. Ukrainians fleeing the war were usually women and children. They were near neighbours geographically and culturally relatively similar. Disentangling these factors is hard.

In summary, race is certainly not the only factor that shapes perceptions of which prospective migrants should be welcomed, but it is clearly one of them.

What to prioritize?

Designing policies to satisfy all policymakers' goals is extremely difficult. The option policymakers think

Figure 2.2: Share of respondents saying they would not want to have immigrants as neighbours

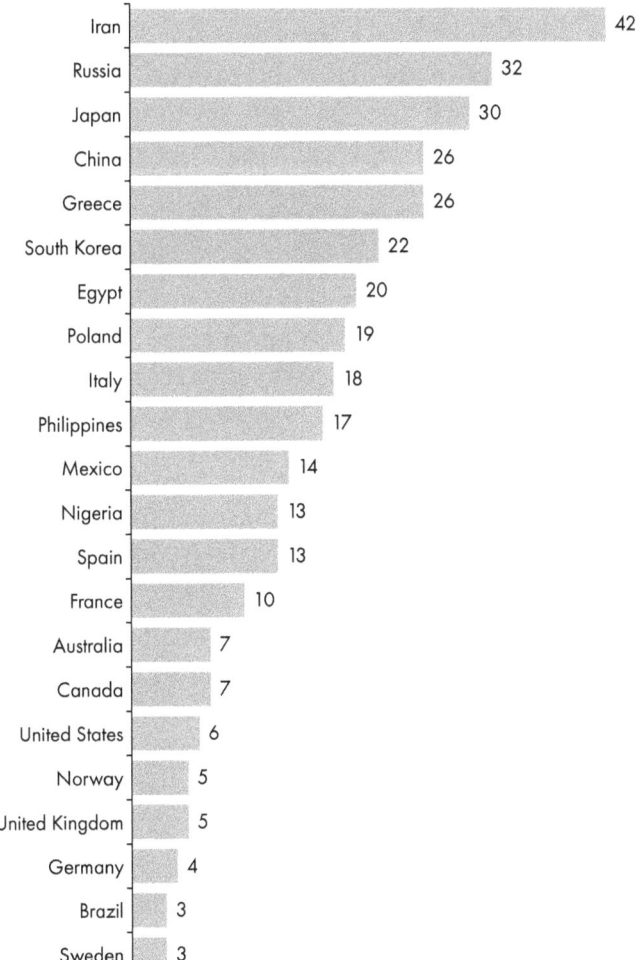

Note: All surveys were conducted between and 2017 and 2022, with individuals aged 18+. British data were collected in 2022. Respondents were given a list of groups, and asked to select all those which they would not like to have as neighbours.

is most ethical may be less economically beneficial. For example, governments often implement work visa policies that tie low-wage workers to a particular employer because they want more control over which jobs migrant workers will do – even though they know this puts migrants at greater risk of exploitation. Similarly, governments often make it hard for people to claim asylum in order to reduce the economic costs and the pace of social change, even if they also believe that a liberal approach would be more ethical.

Politicians' job is to balance these competing concerns. As they do this, they get lobbied from all sides. Some interests are more organized and powerful than others. Some policies attract more attention than others, which leaves scope for 'quiet' policymaking that is less consistent with public opinion if the topic is not too visible.

Nonetheless, I will assume in this book that politicians see all the goals we've discussed as desirable. That is, they want economic growth, social cohesion and security, and they want their policies to be seen as ethical. I'll assume that they either share their voters' views or want their voters to think that they share them. They want to be re-elected.

Policymakers sometimes find it difficult to admit how many constraints they face. And in the political marketplace, certainty is more attractive than doubt – at least in the short run, before it becomes clear that the certainty was misplaced. But saying, 'We don't know whether this will work but we'll try it out and if it fails, we'll try something new' doesn't sound great on the campaign trail.

Often the result is a slightly exaggerated version of the truth: presenting something as a bold solution when really it will only make a difference at the margins. In some cases, though, politicians propose policies that sound good even though there is good evidence they will not work. These are known as symbolic policies – there for show rather than impact.

A classic example is development funding to address the 'root causes' of unauthorized migration. If we invest in prospective migrants' countries of origin, the argument goes, they will be able to live good lives there and won't want to leave. It sounds sensible. But even if development funding successfully raised incomes in countries of origin (a big if), this won't necessarily make people less likely to migrate. People need resources to migrate. More often, migrants come from middle-income regions and middle-class backgrounds. Development funding has merits in its own right. Reducing unauthorized migration from low-income countries probably isn't one of them.

The next few chapters each look at a different area of migration policy, from skilled workers to refugees and unauthorized migrants. In each case, we'll see how policymakers deal with these conflicts and constraints – what they are trying to achieve, and whether they manage it.

3
SKILLED WORK VISAS

'We are pleased that the Government is planning not only to protect the migrant route for investors and entrepreneurs but also to encourage high net worth individuals to come to the UK to drive economic growth', declared the UK's Home Affairs Committee, a cross-party group of MPs, in 2010. Investors and entrepreneurs were widely accepted as being among the most sought-after skilled migrants, even at a time when the UK was restricting many other forms of migration.

A decade later, however, politicians were less than enthusiastic about these visa routes. The Entrepreneur Visa, which had admitted anyone with at least £200,000 in start-up funds, was closed in 2019 on the basis that it had facilitated 'low-quality projects which contributed little or nothing to the UK economy'.[1] In 2022, Home Secretary Priti Patel announced she was abolishing the Investor Visa, which admitted people investing at least £2 million in UK businesses, to stop 'corrupt elites who threaten our national security and push dirty money around our cities'.[2]

High-skilled migration should be one of the easiest areas of immigration policy. It is politically popular. Research consistently suggests that migration's largest economic benefits come people who work in high-skilled jobs. As a result, all high-income countries offer visas for well-paid professionals. Many have particularly liberal rules for jobs they consider most desirable, such as scientists or medical professionals.

However, the example of investor and entrepreneur programmes shows that governments can still face challenges trying to admit the so-called 'brightest and best'. In the UK Investor Visa case, the government discovered that their selection criteria were poorly targeted. Admitting people who were willing to invest a couple of million pounds in a UK business in order to secure a visa was not a good indicator of their ability or intention to become a venture capitalist. Policymakers wanted to attract shrewd captains of industry who would shift parts of their business empires to the UK as they built a new life there. Instead, the typical applicant was a Russian or Chinese housewife whose wealthy husband spent as much time out of the country as they could without losing the visa.[3] Skilled work visa policies can sometimes be more difficult than one might expect.

Who is skilled?

You might think education is a good measure of a person's skill. But education doesn't guarantee people skilled employment, especially if local employers don't recognize their qualifications. As a result, a common stereotype in migration policy debates is the 'PhD taxi driver', overqualified for the work they are doing. Chinese-born molecular biologist Cai Mingjie became famous for a blog documenting his experience as 'Singapore's most educated cab driver'.[4]

For much of the 20th century, the approach to this problem was discretion. Front-line officers would make a subjective judgement about prospective migrants. For example, when the UK 1905 Aliens Act first introduced selection criteria, border officers had to decide whether the person in front of them was a 'lunatic or idiot'. Until the early 2000s, the Canadian points system included an immigration officer's personal assessment of the applicant. Case notes from immigration officials in the late 1950s and 1960s, when this system was being developed, include personal observations on whether applicants were 'hardworking' and 'made a good impression' or came across as 'dishonourable' or displaying a 'bad attitude'.[5]

Caseworker discretion in high-skilled work visa policy has gone out of fashion in many countries, probably for good reason. Can immigration officers make good decisions on who is skilled? They are not obviously qualified for the task. Skilled workers do jobs ranging from nursing and teaching to graphic design and management consultancy. The average government case worker cannot be expected to know much about these things. That's probably why a review of Canada's points system in the late 1990s argued

Figure 3.1: 'I'd call that highly skilled'

"I'd call that 'highly skilled'. It's a 'yes' from me"

that the immigration officer's personal assessment of the applicant completely failed to predict how well skilled migrants actually did in the labour market.[6] Plus they might consciously or unconsciously draw on personal prejudices about applicants' race, gender or other characteristics.

Option one is to remove personal judgement and create a box-ticking exercise instead. In immigration policy, box-ticking has its advantages. Applicants get more certainty if they know precisely what the criteria are. Removing discretion should also reduce the risk of inaccurate decisions informed by prejudice. If we go with this option, the challenge is just to decide which boxes need to be ticked. The best-known example of this approach is the 'points system'.

Are points systems pointless?

The points system was a Canadian innovation from the mid-1960s. Variants were later used in Australia, New Zealand, Austria and the UK. The basic idea is that applicants score points for characteristics like education, language skills and age (younger usually means more points). The people with the most points are invited to apply for a visa. Points can be traded against each other: if your language skills are not too good, you may be able to make up for it with more years of skilled work experience.

People in focus groups or opinion polls tend to like the idea of selecting migrants using points systems. I don't blame them: it sounds rational, scientific and meritocratic. More points sound like a good thing. So the migrants with the most points must be the best ones, right?

The problem is that behind the scientific veneer, it's not clear points systems are any better at selecting skilled migrants than other systems. Indeed, they may be worse. How many points should each characteristic get? How many years of work experience 'makes up for' being graded one level lower on a language test? I don't know, and policymakers don't either – or at least, not with the level of precision that points systems pretend to justify. Points systems have arguably survived not because they work particularly well but because they sound good.

Indeed, despite decades of experience and numerous reviews and adjustments to the criteria, a 2024 review of Australia's points system declared that 'the points test is not delivering for Australia', as it was failing to identify the workers who would be most successful at finding skilled work.[7] It concluded that the system needed to be better 'calibrated'. But perhaps the reality is that this modest tool just can't deliver everything policymakers and the public want from it.

Market solutions

What if the government simply isn't very good at deciding which economic migrants should be admitted? An alternative is to let the market decide.

A radical proposal to remove selection decisions from policymakers is to sell work permits or auction them to the highest bidder. Gary Becker, a Nobel Prize-winning economist from the University of Chicago – the spiritual home of neoclassical economics – famously proposed this idea.[8] For a long time, the idea generated no interest among policymakers in most high-income countries – until US President Donald Trump embraced it with his 'gold card' scheme in his second term.

Becker wanted higher levels of immigration to the US but worried that open borders would undermine the welfare state because there was no guarantee that migrants would be able to support themselves. He proposed that selling visas would attract the people who had most to gain from migrating and who were most committed to the country. Meanwhile, the revenues could go towards reducing the tax burden on Americans, mitigating public opposition to migration. A loan system could enable people from low-income backgrounds to participate.

This proposal is a bit naïve. Becker believed a fee would attract young, skilled people who could earn much more in the US than in their home country. In practice, the experience with investor visas in high-income countries – which I described earlier – suggests what would actually happen: very wealthy people with no plans to work would happily pay the fee and treat it as a leisure visa. Under an auction model, wealthy leisure migrants would quickly price out the aspiring Americans from developing countries whom Becker imagined using the programme.

Nonetheless, some countries have quietly introduced a variant of this policy by charging high fees on top of their existing selection policies. In 2024, UK work visas were among the most expensive worldwide, followed by Australian.[9] For example, a worker moving to the UK with his or her partner to take up a coding job in 2025 would eventually expect to pay almost £20,000 in government fees from their initial entry visas to permanent settlement, not including fees charged to their employer. The UK has raked in a lot of revenue, and the Treasury no doubt appreciates that. However, it is not obvious that it has had any impact on public attitudes towards migration, as Becker suggested (although perhaps he would argue that the price was simply too low).

A less radical method of using the market to decide who migrates is already ubiquitous across high-income countries, however: outsourcing the decision to employers.

Officials may not have the expertise to know who is employable, but employers certainly do. Employers spend a lot of time trying to recruit people with the skills they want. Staff with specialized knowledge review job applications and interview candidates. And they are willing to do all this at no cost to the government. In fact, they are even willing to pay a fee for the privilege, to get their preferred candidate a work visa.

Compared with this detailed and resource-intensive process, making government officials select workers by totting up scores in response to a few questions on a points test seems absurd.

But before we get carried away with the benefits of employer sponsorship, there are – as always – trade-offs. What if we don't trust employers? What if they want to hire workers from abroad not because they have exceptional skills but because they accept lower wages or are easier to exploit? Or what if employers' interests conflict with the broader social good?

These are all risks. When it comes to high-skilled migration they can mostly be mitigated. In the next chapter, I will talk about the widespread problem of exploitation in employer-sponsored visas. The evidence isn't definitive, but the more skilled and better paid the roles, the more comfortable we can generally feel about outsourcing selection decisions to employers. People in highly skilled jobs will usually have reasonably good language skills and should be better able to find out what their rights are. Perhaps most importantly, they will be able to shop around for another job if they don't like the way their employer treats them. Some employers will still take advantage of sponsored skilled workers, but the power imbalance is less severe than it is in low-wage jobs. Policymakers worried about exploitation can make it as easy as possible to switch their visa to a new employer.

Policymakers can also mitigate the risk that employers will not worry about the broader impacts on society when recruiting workers. They can impose their own selection criteria too. For example, many countries require people on work visas to pass language tests even if the employers don't require them to.

Employer sponsorship is not perfect. It doesn't cover everyone: for example, freelancers and entrepreneurs are often excluded. Policymakers with liberal attitudes towards migration sometimes worry that they will not get enough skilled migrants by relying on employer sponsorship alone. But there's a good reason that it is ubiquitous across high-income countries, even in countries that *also* have points systems: it works well enough.

Are countries competing for talent?

So far in this chapter, I have assumed that many skilled people want to migrate and that destination countries' main job is to decide whom to accept or refuse. That is broadly true in popular destinations like the US, the UK or Australia. It's less true in some high-income countries like Italy or Greece, which have attracted unusually low shares of degree-educated migrants.[10]

Enter the rhetoric about the need for a competitive offer to skilled migrants in the 'global race for talent'. Perhaps surprisingly, we hear this rhetoric even in the countries that appear to be winning said race.

'America needs smart immigration reforms to win the race for global talent', declared US businessman and politician David McCormick, for example, in a 2021 column.[11] Anyone who works on immigration policy will be quite familiar with this line. If they don't come here, the argument goes, some other country will scoop them up, and then ... well ... that would be bad, right?

The idea of the global race for talent sounds intuitive if you don't spend too long thinking it through. It relies on three main assumptions. First, that people pick and choose between multiple countries. Second, that immigration policy plays a meaningful role in their decisions. And, third, that one more skilled worker for us means one fewer for Germany, Australia or wherever – that is, attracting workers is what economists call a zero-sum game.

These things are often not true. There is evidence that international students choose between countries, and visa policies matter to at least some of them (for example, the right to work after studying).[12] Businesses may compete for talent with other businesses, including companies outside of the country, so they are understandably irritated when immigration policies stand in their way. (Note that sometimes the policies that stand in their way are simply preventing them from paying pretty low wages to workers they claim are exceptionally skilled.)

But for the most part, we should be sceptical that competition for skilled workers is a zero-sum game. Migrants are not widgets to be distributed between countries. Many are only willing or able to go to one place. Language barriers and networks greatly narrow their options. If people fail to get a slot in the US skilled worker visa lottery,* some will look for options in Canada or Germany, but many will simply stay in their country of origin.

Finally, immigration policies do not necessarily play a decisive role in where people go. People move for opportunities, not for a good visa regulation.[13] Making visas more attractive might have impacts at the margins, but it will be less important than the fundamentals, namely whether the country is a good place for migrants to live and work. Before the immigration rule-makers even put pen to paper, their room for manoeuvre has been greatly constrained by factors well beyond their control.

The main challenge governments face is to design rules that make sense in their own right – regardless

---

* Yes, the US issues work visas by lottery. Its cap on sought-after 'H-1B visas' is perennially oversubscribed, and rather than selecting who gets visas in a strategic way, the US resorts to random selection.

of what other countries are doing. Many countries choose liberal policies for the highest-skilled workers, exempting them from caps and bureaucracy that may apply in other work visa categories. For example, the US caps its skilled worker 'H-1B' visa, but exempts university researchers from the cap. It has no limit on a separate category of visas for people who can convince the immigration agency they have 'extraordinary ability'. Singapore allows the highest earning migrants to work in the country without being tied to a sponsoring employer. In my experience, governments introduce policies like this not because they need to be more liberal than some competitor country, but because they think it is a good idea.

Brain drain

If we are not competing with other destinations for skilled workers, are we competing with countries of origin? Enter the 'brain drain' debate – arguably the most important criticism of high-skilled migration.

The impacts of brain drain are complex.[14] For a long time, scholars argued that emigration (that is, people migrating away from a country) denudes origin communities of their most talented people. Losing highly skilled workers can undermine public finances, because higher-paid workers pay more tax. Origin countries lose the investment they made in young adults' education if they emigrate. Having fewer skilled people may make it harder to develop knowledge-intensive industries. Countries also lose educated citizens who might have contributed to civic life, democratic institutions or the arts.

Concerns about losing skilled workers are especially acute when it comes to essential workers like doctors and nurses. Many developing countries have faced chronic shortages of health professionals, particularly in sub-Saharan Africa.[15] Some are also major countries of emigration, such as Nigeria. These shortages put patients at risk and make it harder to improve public health, which in turn is important to economic and societal development.[16] A 2011 study found that the lost investment from training doctors in Zimbabwe and South Africa as a result of emigration to Australia, Canada, the UK and the US exceeded US$100,000 per doctor (not accounting for inflation since then).[17]

There is also another side to this coin, however. Emigration can benefit countries of origin in some circumstances. Emigrants don't always disappear forever: some create international networks that bring home new ideas and business opportunities. Migrant inventors still collaborate with people in their countries of origin.[18] Other workers send remittances to family and friends at home. In 2022, personal remittances made up more than 20 percent of gross domestic product in quite a few countries around the world, including Lebanon, Nepal and Honduras.[19]

The number of skilled people in origin countries is not fixed. The opportunity to emigrate may give people a greater incentive to pursue education.[20] Some people acquire skills hoping they will emigrate, but never do.[21] This beneficial impact on education at home won't necessarily take place everywhere, though – it depends on whether the countries have the capacity to expand education to meet demand.

Some governments explicitly encourage emigration. The Philippines, for example, has long had explicit policies for sending nurses overseas, as part of a strategy to generate remittances.[22] India and Turkey seek visa opportunities for their citizens in trade agreements. However, many origin countries see emigration as an economic and cultural loss. While they cannot usually prevent people from leaving, India and Mexico require international students who received government funding to return for a minimum period. Others, such as Italy and Portugal, have offered tax incentives for their nationals abroad to return home.

It is hard to say how the costs and benefits of emigration add up overall. The impacts will probably vary quite a lot by country. Countries with weak institutions and very low living standards are probably least well equipped to take advantage of the benefits of being better networked in the global economy, though they may benefit the most from remittances. The costs of emigration probably outweigh the benefits in the case of health professionals.

If brain drain is an ethical problem, what can immigration policymakers do about it? Radical approaches might prevent people from migrating from lower-income countries, denying them visas. This is ethically complicated. Origin countries do not own their citizens, even if they have invested in their education in the short run. The Kenyan entrepreneur,

Lydiah Kemunto Bosire, argues that the brain drain narrative patronizes people from low-income countries by suggesting that 'Africans belong in Africa' and shouldn't be allowed the same opportunities as people from South Korea or Germany.[23]

An alternative to banning emigration would be for high-income countries to fund education in origin countries, given that they benefit from it. In practice, most are not going to want to do this in any meaningful way. After all, not having to pay for skilled workers' education is one of the things that makes skilled migration attractive and economically beneficial. One migration scholar suggested getting around this problem by taxing skilled emigrants themselves and routing the funds to development aid,[24] although this proposal raises logistical and political challenges and has not had any traction in practice.

The onus may thus end up being on origin countries to mitigate the damage – for example, by providing student loans that require people to work in their country of origin for a minimum period after graduation. Destination countries do sometimes cooperate in this effort. For example, the US prevents some students with origin government-funded scholarships from switching to long-term work visas, unless they first returned home for at least two years.

What is skilled work visa policy for?

I started with skilled work visas because it is the easiest area of immigration policy. High-skilled work migration tends to be politically popular. The economic benefits are well established. It makes up a relatively small share of overall migration in high-income countries. It's thus no surprise that policies towards skilled migrants tend to be on the more liberal end of the spectrum.

However, there are still challenges. Migration routes designed to admit skilled migrants don't always work. Some end up admitting highly educated people who struggle to find skilled work. The more unusual a person's skills, the harder it is to design a coherent programme to admit them.

While high-skilled work migration is the category policymakers tend to like most, it is also the easiest to cut if *something* is to be cut. Policymakers often struggle to reduce asylum or family migration – for a host of practical, ethical and legal reasons that we will encounter throughout this book. By contrast, high-skilled migration is relatively controllable. In practice, policymakers can face a trade-off between the desire to reap economic benefits from admitting skilled workers from overseas and the desire to reduce overall migration. We'll come back to this point in the last chapter.

4
LOW-WAGE WORK

James works in finance. He is one of the 'highly skilled' migrants we discussed in the previous chapter. His employer needs someone to run a new team in Singapore, and he takes up the offer. His firm handles the immigration paperwork and he breezes through passport control with his wife and children a few weeks later. If he wants to become a permanent resident, he can – but he doesn't fancy mandatory National Service, so he decides not to.

Things aren't so easy for his maid, Maria. She has come from the Philippines on a domestic worker visa. She can't bring her husband or children, who remain at home. If she wants to move to another employer, she needs James' permission. Even if she lives in the country for decades, she will not be eligible for permanent residence. She's willing to put up with this because she can earn a lot more in Singapore than she would at home, and her family depend on the remittances.

The details vary by country, but the basic trend is clear: immigration policies treat workers in high-skilled jobs much more generously. Low-wage workers have fewer migration options. And if they can get a work visa, they typically enjoy fewer rights, such as the ability to get a secure permanent status, switch between employers or bring family members with them. This chapter looks at why.

Why have low-wage work visas?

'Employers are struggling to fill vacancies' is one of the common arguments for low-wage work visas in public debates. Advocates and employer associations in industries like hospitality, construction, retail and haulage frequently point to unfilled vacancies as an argument for migration. But just because there are vacancies, must policymakers provide work visas to fill them? Not necessarily. The economic arguments for migration into low-wage jobs are much less convincing than at the top end of the pay and skills spectrum.

Migration is good for employers in sectors that rely on low-wage workers, such as retail, hospitality, food processing, childcare, and services like cleaning or beauty salons. With more workers, employers can expand their businesses despite offering relatively poor pay and conditions. For example, the expansion of the European Union (EU) in 2004 brought many more EU workers to the UK who were willing to do low-wage, labour-intensive jobs such as making Pret coffees or picking asparagus. One result is that UK farms started to plant more asparagus.[1]

In theory, expanding low-wage sectors in this way can benefit consumers by making services available more widely and at lower cost. In practice, the impacts of migration on prices appears to be small, although there may be exceptions in sectors that rely on migrant workers most.[2] For example, one US study found that highly skilled American women worked more hours in cities with larger migrant populations, because they purchased more housekeeping and childcare.[3]

At the same time, migration into low-wage jobs has costs. Employers benefit in the short term, but may face less pressure to adopt labour-saving technology such as machinery for harvesting or food processing in the longer term.[4] Migration shifts the composition of the economy slightly towards labour-intensive, low-productivity industries. This is not obviously a good thing, although economists tend not to have strong views on precisely how big each sector of the economy should be.

The 'price of rights'

The impacts of migration into low-wage jobs depend quite a lot on the rights migrant workers are given. Workers on short-term work visas are typically not eligible for welfare benefits. They are tied to an employer and if they lose their job, they are required to go home. They often cannot bring family members with them. The visa will typically be strictly temporary with no option to become a permanent resident.

All this can make people in low-wage work visa programmes vulnerable. Exploitation is endemic. For example, the US agricultural worker visa has seen repeated reports over many years of employers failing to pay wages, providing unsafe housing or working conditions, and even sexual harassment.[5] When the UK opened up a route for care workers in 2022, it saw extraordinary levels of abuse, with workers forced into conditions akin to slavery. These experiences are not unique.

At the same time, programmes that prevent access to permanent status rely on a constant churn of newcomers who cannot stay permanently. On average, migrants participating in the programmes will have less

Figure 4.1: Mexican agricultural labourers topping sugar beets in 1943 near Stockton, California

local knowledge and language skills, because these are things that build up over time. Integration is 'designed out' of the system.

So why do governments often decide *not* to give low-wage work visa holders a secure immigration status with more rights? As migration scholar Martin Ruhs has pointed out, rights have a price.[6] If a person is only allowed to spend a short time in the country, cannot access welfare benefits, and cannot bring their children or non-working partner, the costs are minimal. However, the costs of supporting people in low-wage jobs increase over time, regardless of nationality, as people get older and especially once they retire. Families with an adult who doesn't work are much more likely to present a fiscal cost than ones with two working adults. As we saw in Chapter 2, workers on low incomes present a fiscal cost in the long run.

From a social perspective, adding to the population of people on low incomes in the long run can also has drawbacks. For example, children who grow up near or below the poverty line face many forms of disadvantage throughout their lives. Low incomes make it harder for people to participate fully in society, especially if people also lack language skills.

Perhaps the most common approach high-income countries have taken in response is to restrict low-wage migrant workers' rights in an attempt to reduce the costs.

Understandably, opinions are divided on whether to do this. The US open borders advocate Bryan Caplan argues that *permanently* preventing immigrants to the US from accessing welfare benefits, or even permanently taxing them at a higher rate, is still a great deal for migrants if it means Americans allow more people to migrate.

On the other hand, restricting rights long term risks creating an underclass of economic migrants. In the United Arab Emirates, non-citizens can spend decades toiling in construction sites or hotels without a route to citizenship for themselves or their children. There is an economic logic to it and the privileged minority who are citizens of the country benefit from low-cost goods and services. But it's not the kind of society

Box 4.1: Tying workers to employers

Governments often decide they want to minimize low-wage work migration, but welcome migrant workers in jobs where they think there is a specific need, such as seasonal agriculture, construction or care work. Tying workers to particular jobs and employers helps them do this by ensuring migrant workers are doing the 'right' jobs.

But there is a trade-off. Employer sponsorship gives employers more power over their workers. Some will use their advantage to underpay them and threaten them with deportation should they complain. Low-wage migrants are already vulnerable to exploitation, regardless of their immigration status. Employer-sponsored work visas can exacerbate this problem.

everyone wants to live in. One thing that makes the Gulf countries' immigration model unpalatable to many onlookers from Western democracies – in addition to the exceptionally high levels of immigration they permit – is that migrants can live there for decades without gaining anything close to the rights enjoyed by citizens.

Restrictions on rights may feel more justifiable for short periods, but the longer people stay, the more they come to be considered – and consider themselves – part of society.

Do high-income countries need low-wage work migration at all?

Policymakers face a trade-off: restrict rights and increase the risk of exploitation; grant rights and increase the risk of financial costs. A third option is for policymakers to wash their hands of low-wage work visa programmes entirely. Is this a sustainable option, or do high-income countries *need* these programmes?

Without work visas in low-wage jobs, there would still be migrant workers. Many workers in low-wage jobs such as food processing, elder care or hospitality arrive as family members or refugees. However, work visa programmes make the number of workers larger.

Limiting migration into low-wage work arguably only really causes problems when policymakers have *non-economic* reasons for wanting people to consume more of the goods or services that low-wage workers produce. There is no optimal number of lattes the public should consume (putting aside the health impacts of too much caffeine). But it does matter whether elderly people have decent care, or whether the cost of childcare is prohibitive for working parents. Producing at least some food here rather than importing it all from abroad reduces our risks in the face of future shocks. For these reasons, many countries give privileged access to visas for low-wage workers in agriculture, social care and childcare – although often only short term, in order to avoid the fiscal costs.

Interestingly, the labour or skills shortages that people worry most about are sometimes in publicly funded or subsidized sectors, such as teaching, health or social care. They are publicly funded because governments consider them particularly important. But public funding is inevitably limited. The result is low wages and jobs that struggle to attract recruits. While policymakers like to tell employers that they should invest in local workers instead of recruiting from overseas, they are not innocent themselves.

In the very short run, admitting people who are willing to work in low-paid publicly funded jobs such as care may save some money. In the longer run, the fiscal costs of long-term migration into low-wage jobs may be a false economy – at least if workers are ultimately able to receive a secure, permanent immigration status that does not tie them to the care sector.

Box 4.2: Does demographic decline require low-wage migration?

Ageing populations are a huge problem for high-income countries. Wealthy countries use taxes from people who are working now to support people who are not working. If the retired population grows and the working-age population doesn't, there is less tax money to go around. This threatens the financial stability of pensions systems and the welfare state.

Is immigration the solution? The scale of immigration that would be needed to prevent the share of older people per worker from increasing is very large. In Canada, for example, one projection found that even if immigration increased to 1.8 percent of the entire population for 50 years – enough to more than double the population from just under 40 million to approaching 100 million – the number of retirees supported by every 100 workers would still rise sharply from roughly 30 to around 40 (compared to just over 50 in the scenario with annual immigration at 0.9 percent of the population).[7] Projections in the UK and the Netherlands have found similarly small effects.[8] In sum, immigration may help mitigate some of the challenges of population ageing, particularly in countries facing the prospect of population collapse due to ultra-low fertility, such as South Korea. But it has less impact than many people assume.

Population growth itself has other benefits and costs. Bringing people together in densely populated cities can bring economic benefits.[9] At the same time, countries that struggle to build enough houses to keep up with their population size may see upwards pressure on housing costs. Population growth means we need more infrastructure such as roads, schools and hospitals. All this must be built and someone has to pay for it.[10] When newcomers are working in highly paid jobs and paying a lot in tax, finding the money for a bit more infrastructure investment isn't too difficult.

One problem with demographic arguments is that they often encourage us to focus too much on how much migration there is and not *who* is migrating. Population ageing is mostly a public finances problem. We need enough people working and paying tax to support the retired population. Adding people to the working-age population thus only helps public finances if they are paying more in tax than it costs to provide them with public services and any welfare benefits. That implies that policymakers worried about demographic change should focus on admitting people who will work in relatively high-paid jobs, rather than increasing migration across the board.

An exception to this rule is that ageing populations will require more care, and someone has to provide it. Whether that should mean recruiting more workers from overseas is a complicated question, though, as I discuss further in what follows.

Population growth is not just an economic question. For example, Canada's Century Initiative, an advocacy group,

> has argued that a larger population will increase the country's influence on the world stage. Indeed, population growth due to generations of high migration is one of the reasons the US today commands huge influence and around a quarter of the global economy.
>
> On the other hand, population growth can have drawbacks. While it is possible to inhabit cities more densely, population growth sometimes instead leads to urban sprawl with new building on green spaces.

The politics of low-wage work migration

Opinion polls show a strong preference for high-skilled over low-skilled migration.[11] Immigration policies that are perceived as skill-selective appear to gain public acceptance more easily.[12]

This is broadly in line with the economic evidence, which suggests that migration into high-skilled jobs tends to bring benefits, and migration into low-wage work more likely to bring costs.

The politics of low-wage work migration is complicated, however. When economists talk about the economy, they tend to focus on standard metrics like public finances, the labour market, and prices of goods, services and housing. As a policy person, this is also how I like to think about the economy. But other people have different ideas about which types of migration have positive economic impacts. In particular, people don't always make a clear distinction between whether a worker has a positive economic impact and whether they seem to be a nice person.

For example, one group of workers that most economists would wave through without a second thought is bankers. Financial services workers earn a lot and their fiscal contributions subsidize the rest of us. But in a 2023 poll,[13] respondents supported reducing the number of bankers admitted, even though they were happy to see higher numbers of restaurant staff and lorry drivers.* Many people see finance as an unworthy enterprise, or see bankers as ruthless and overpaid. These views about which occupations are morally or socially desirable are also reflected in attitudes towards immigration policy.

In one striking poll, respondents were 21 percentage points more likely to say that a hypothetical Nigerian building contractor was making a meaningful contribution to the UK economy if they were also told he had become a UK citizen.[14] But citizenship is a cultural and social question, and has only small impacts on migrants' economic contribution.

---

* I wondered if the word 'bankers' biased the results, since it is associated with things like 'bankers' bonuses'. When my colleagues and I designed a 2022 survey, we asked about 'financial sector workers' rather than 'bankers'. Respondents were not fooled. They still ranked them lowest of the pack, below farm workers, waiters and lorry drivers.

Box 4.3: Shortage occupation lists and the technocratic dream

'The [shortage occupation list will ensure] Australia has a targeted skilled migration system that addresses genuine skills gaps in the economy', declared the Australian skills minister, Andrew Giles, in 2024.[15] Such statements are common in the numerous countries that have special lists of occupations that get easier access to the work-visa system.

The idea of targeting work migration at occupations where there are shortages sounds appealing: rational, evidence-based and scientific. The reality is disappointing. Policymakers are not omniscient. It's incredibly difficult to know where the shortages are in a labour market with hundreds of occupations covering everything from air traffic controllers and librarians to upholsterers and video-game makers. It is equally difficult to adjust immigration policy in a sensible way to address any shortages.

The widespread use of policies aimed at addressing shortages arguably responds to a political rationale, rather than an economic one. People enjoy the comforting fiction that work visas are carefully calibrated to the needs of the economy. But there's a good chance that the occupations on the list – based on data or someone's subjective judgements months or sometimes years ago – are not actually the ones where employers find it hardest to recruit. And even if they are, immigration policy will not always be the right solution.

> Shortages come and go, and the ones that stick around in the lower half of the labour market are often caused by problems outside of the immigration system, such as poor pay and conditions – problems that immigration policy doesn't fix in the long run.

What is low-wage work visa policy for?

Governments tend to restrict low-wage work visas, allowing it in cases where they consider it really necessary. Deciding what is 'necessary' is a subjective exercise: beware of experts who tell you there is an obvious evidence-based answer to this question. In practice, low-wage work visa policies often admit people who will produce goods and services that governments want their populations to consume more of but don't want to finance too heavily. That may include anything from elder care and childcare to locally grown fruit and vegetables.

This chapter has examined low-wage work visa programmes in isolation. However, the broader context is important. Many countries experience migration into low-wage jobs through other immigration routes, such as family members and refugees. Even if low-wage work routes are very restrictive, there will still be at least some workers coming through other routes.

As the next chapters will show, family and asylum routes are harder to restrict than low-wage work visas, much as some policymakers would like to do so. As a result, policymakers who want to reduce overall migration – for social, political or economic reasons – will often find that low-wage work visas are the easiest category to cut. That's one reason why relatively few of them exist in the first place.

5
FAMILY MIGRATION

In the 1990s Hollywood romcom *Green Card*, Brontë and Georges, an unlikely couple, enter a marriage of convenience so that Georges can stay in the US after his tourist visa expires. This being a romcom, they eventually fall in love for real, but only after the immigration officers uncover their deceit. When officers visit them at home, Georges is caught out: he cannot find the bathroom in the flat they supposedly share. In a follow-up interview, he breaks down and confesses to the fraudulent marriage after failing to remember the name of his wife's face cream.

The film may have taken a few liberties, but the immigration process it described is more or less realistic. Many countries interview couples separately if they suspect the relationship may not be genuine. That is labour-intensive, so more often caseworkers make decisions based on the paperwork, which might include proof of living together as a couple, or even WhatsApp exchanges and letters from friends.

Most people in genuine relationships will sail through this process, although there are exceptions. For example, 'unlikely' couples naturally tend to arouse more suspicion, such as an older woman marrying a younger, non-citizen man.[1] Indeed, immigration officers sometimes warn women in apparently unusual relationships that the partner may be taking advantage of them in order to secure immigration status.[2] A couple who meet on holiday abroad, fall in love and marry a few weeks later without ever having lived together in the same country can be hard to distinguish from a marriage conducted purely to secure a visa.

Nonetheless, proving the relationship is real tends not to be the biggest barrier to securing a spouse visa. In my experience, many people assume that being in a genuine relationship with a citizen is sufficient to qualify you for residence or even immediate citizenship. Moral philosophers also argue for allowing people to live with their partner and children in the place they consider home.[3]

In reality, many countries allow family migration only reluctantly. Policymakers once again juggle competing objectives. One goal is to enable families to live together – either because policymakers value family life, or because human rights laws tell them they must. However, policymakers often also want to restrict family migration that will present economic costs or that they believe will bring undesired social or cultural change.

How to strike the balance between these competing objectives is a dilemma for politicians, but it has also become a legal question: family migration is one of several areas of immigration policy where human rights law has played a substantial role.

This chapter focuses on partner migration: the most common form of family migration. Before looking at the impacts of partner migration policies, some brief history.

How did we get here?

In the late 19th and early 20th centuries, immigration policies in today's high-income countries were relatively liberal so there was no need for a specific family visa. Migrants arriving in Ellis Island around the turn of the century, for example, came for work, family and refuge. The government did not scrutinize migrants' motivations, but excluded people for specific reasons such as health conditions or risk of poverty.

As immigration rules became more restrictive during the 20th century, there was pressure to carve out specific rules for family unification. For example, during the economic downturn in Europe in the early 1970s, many governments restricted work migration. However, family migration continued to be permitted, whether for ethical or legal reasons.[4]

Since family unification had become one of the few remaining legal migration pathways, its role in overall immigration became more significant. Policymakers had not anticipated the long legacy of family migration that would continue even after work migration was restricted. Governments' attitude to family migration is nicely summed up by Swiss novelist Max Frisch's famous 1965 quote: 'We wanted workers, but we got people instead.'

Family migration did not only involve the guest workers who had arrived in the post-war period. As other links between countries, such as trade and tourism, grew, personal connections across borders meant that new families were formed. Some families included naturalized migrants or children of migrants who married someone from their country of heritage. Others involved citizens with no migration background marrying people they met abroad or online, or a person who had already migrated for work or study.

While many high-income countries initially had relatively liberal family policies, family migration attracted more scrutiny as its importance in immigration systems grew. In the 1990s and 2000s, many European countries such as the Netherlands, Germany and Denmark introduced restrictions such as civics tests, language requirements and income thresholds.[5] Policy has not moved exclusively in a restrictive direction, however. Human rights laws have sometimes forced governments to take a more liberal position than they would have liked.

While these measures reduced family migration, it remains the largest source of permanent migration in most high-income countries today.[6] Almost half of foreign-born people in European Union (EU) countries in 2021 said that they had originally migrated for family reasons, for example.[7] Most are partners (see Box 5.1).

Box 5.1: Who is eligible for family visas?

This chapter focuses on policies that regulate a country's own citizens' ability to bring a foreign partner to the country. All high-income countries offer partner visas, even if they impose some restrictions.

Rules on family members other than partners vary. For example, the US has liberal rules for bringing in parents, while the UK only allows parents to migrate in exceptional cases where suitable care is not available overseas. In general, high-income countries tend not to allow citizens to sponsor visas for siblings, aunts and uncles, or nieces and nephews, although there are exceptions. For example, Canada's 'lonely Canadian' rule allows people with no other blood relatives in the country to sponsor one blood relative such as a cousin, aunt or uncle.

Separate policies govern migration of family members to accompany *other migrants* on work or study visas. These rules are often more restrictive. Temporary seasonal work or youth 'backpacker' visas, for example, often do not allow people to bring any family members with them. To some extent, these restrictions are ethically less complicated than family migration policies for citizens, because people coming on work and study visas can choose not to migrate in the first place if they find the conditions too restrictive.

Family life

The main goal of partner visas is to enable citizens to live with their spouses in their country of citizenship. If a couple cannot get a partner visa, the consequences for them will depend on their situation. In a best-case scenario, they may be able to live happily in another country. Many simply do not want to live somewhere else, however. Citizens refused partner visas often report feeling betrayed or exiled by their country of birth.[8]

In a minority of cases, the partner's country of citizenship may not allow them to migrate either. For example, in early 2025 UK media reported the story of a 29-year-old British man separated from his Tanzanian partner and British child because neither country would offer the couple a visa.[9] (The UK had income requirements and Tanzania did not have a defined procedure for allowing women to sponsor a male partner.)[10]

Couples who cannot secure partner visas and are not willing or able to live together abroad sometimes live apart. Separation can be a major source of stress, even if it is temporary (for example, if one partner needs to spend time working to become eligible).[11] Separation can make a couple's economic situation more precarious, given that the costs of living alone are higher.

Things get particularly difficult for couples with children, as one adult has to solo-parent the children. There is substantial evidence that growing up in a single-parent household can be bad for children's development.[12] At the same time, the absent partner cannot sustain a normal parental relationship with their child. Research by a children's charity in the UK found that children of couples separated by immigration policies reported anxiety and guilt about the family's situation.[13]

In theory, these problems would not arise if people avoided getting into relationships with people who do not qualify for visas. This might actually happen in some specific cases. For example, one study of British Pakistani families documents how couples would sometimes delay cohabitation and the final stages of the community marriage celebrations until after the prospective migrant's partner visa was approved, to protect the bride from becoming an 'immigration widow' – married but denied a visa.[14] A study of six EU countries suggested that restrictive family migration policies had in fact led some adult children of migrants to find partners who did not require visas.[15] However, many people entering relationships have no idea what the immigration rules say, and by the time they do it is too late.

As a result, not being eligible for partner visas can be a pretty bad outcome for families themselves – especially when the couple already has children. Policymakers who want to restrict partner migration need to justify it by showing that restricting family migration has benefits. Two main justifications arise in practice: economic and social.

Economics and partner migration

Partners are not selected based on their skills or job prospects. They include a wide spectrum of people. Some would outperform the average work visa holder, while others will struggle economically. In many countries, family migrants are less likely to have a job than people who originally arrived on work or study visas, and they tend to work in lower-paid occupations.[16]

It is reasonable to assume that migration of low-income family members will have a negative impact on broad measures like public finances or gross domestic product per person in the long run.

Partners may still contribute to their household's wellbeing and financial stability if they do not work, for example by caring for children or elderly parents. This will enable the other partner to work and reduce the family's reliance on social assistance.

However, from a purely economic perspective, these contributions will often still be smaller than the costs, if migrating partners have low or zero earnings. That is because families in the bottom half of the income distribution tend to pay less tax than it costs to provide them with public services, regardless of their nationality. Even if the immigration system restricts their access to benefits, a lot of public spending is not on welfare benefits, but other things such as healthcare. Total government expenditure in high-income countries tends to be around US$20,000 to US$40,000 per person per annum.[17]

Non-citizen partners joining the lowest-income families will also be at risk of poverty, which has broader social and economic costs.

Balancing economics and family life

So how should policymakers balance the economic cost of some family migration with the human cost of keeping families apart? This question is bitterly disputed. Some argue that citizens' ability to live at home with their partner is a basic freedom everyone deserves, regardless of income. For example, the academic Chris Bertram proposes that if it is not acceptable to deny low-income citizens the right to vote or be protected from crime by the police, it is also wrong to deny them family visas if they marry a non-citizen.[18]

Others hold that economic restrictions are justified because, while people have the right to marry whomever they choose, they do not have the right to bring them to the country at their fellow citizens' expense.

There is no clear science telling policymakers precisely how to strike the right balance between economics and family life. Some countries have very few restrictions on partner migration, such as Australia and Canada. Others set income and language requirements. These requirements are usually not high enough to eliminate all economic costs, but typically focus on excluding families who would be on the lowest incomes. For example, as of 2025 the US required people to have a household income at least 25 percent above the poverty line. The Dutch income requirement was equivalent to a full-time job at the country's (relatively high) minimum wage. As of early 2025, the UK was an outlier among high-income countries, with a minimum income requirement of £29,000, which means that just under half of employed British residents would not have earned enough to meet it.[19]

The balance between the state's right to impose economic restrictions and the individual's right to family life is one of the areas of immigration policy where human rights law constrains some governments' decisions. The European Convention on Human Rights (ECHR) allows governments to create some barriers to families living together, but not if there are 'exceptional circumstances' that would make it 'unduly harsh' (see Box 5.2), which of course leaves room for interpretation.

Box 5.2: Exceptional circumstances

Caroline met her husband Carlos while travelling and working in Ecuador, and returned to the UK for the birth of their child. After the birth, she suffered from post-natal depression. They had assumed that because they were married with a child and Caroline was a UK citizen, Carlos could get a residence visa. But Caroline could not work due to her illness, Carlos wasn't allowed to work, and together they did not meet the UK's income requirement, which at the time was £18,600. After

> a legal challenge, a judge decided their circumstances were sufficiently exceptional that Carlos should receive a visa.[20]
>
> By contrast, Richmond met his British wife and stepson while in the UK on a visit visa and married a few months later.[21] When their family visa was refused, the couple argued that they could not relocate to Ghana, Richmond's country of origin. She had lived in the UK her whole life, had two other adult children there, and her youngest child was about to start school in the UK. She said she would struggle to find work in Ghana without speaking the local language. The judge said that it would not be unreasonable for them to relocate and stay in touch with the UK family through 'modern means of communication' (such as Zoom).

Values and 'social integration'

Criticisms of family migration are often cultural and social, rather than economic. That is, they focus on whether family migration admits 'the right sort' of people into the right sort of families.

Dealing with social and cultural impacts in family migration policy is a bit of a minefield. As I argued in Chapter 2, meaningful differences do exist between migrant and non-migrant populations but deciding which differences matter and why is highly subjective; the differences are only averages and many people don't fit the stereotypes; and policymakers often do not have very precise tools to deal with them.

All of this applies to family migration in spades. An example is the debate about transnational marriages between people of the same religion and ethnicity. Critics argue that some men prefer to find a wife who grew up in a more traditional environment where women are less assertive so that they can avoid adopting social norms such as gender equality. This critique appears to be levelled most often at Muslims, but sometimes also at older White men. Arranged marriages in particular are sometimes criticized for reducing women's choice about whom to marry.

The evidence is complicated. For example, some research in Europe found that a desire for a wife who adheres to more traditional gender norms or religious views has in fact been one of several motivations for some men seeking out transnational marriages, but it is by no means the only one.[22] In the case of arranged marriages, the strength of parents' authority to determine who their children marry appears to be declining, and research suggests that most couples enter into these marriages freely.[23]

Social critiques of marriage migration often focus on specific national or religious groups, particularly Muslims. 'Transnational' marriages often attract less attention when they involve White partners in majority-White countries, even if the motivations are similar. Higher-income groups also find it easier to avoid being criticized for low social integration. A study of German policymakers' attitudes towards family migration found they were much less worried about the social and cultural integration of high-income

Japanese migrants. They might keep themselves to themselves, but in the words of one German official, 'they are all economically so well off, they don't need any integration'. After all, they take care of their children's education and go to the opera.[24]

Finally, policymakers who want to select newcomers based on potential social and cultural impacts face the challenge that the traits they are interested in are difficult to identify in transparent immigration rules.

A UK government consultation back in 2002 indicated the government's dislike of arranged transnational marriages between people of the same ethnicity, for example. It said there was 'a discussion to be had within those communities that continue the practice of arranged marriages as to whether more of these could be undertaken within the settled community here'.[25] But the consultation proposed no further action. As long as a couple enters into their marriage freely, no sensible regulation can specify what degree of parental approval it is acceptable for them to have sought – whether for ethnic minorities or anyone else.

Similarly, policymakers cannot reasonably create selection criteria to screen out women whom they consider excessively submissive, even if they thought that doing so was ethical and legal. (In the past, some tried a blanket approach. In the early 20th century, for example, American women who married non-citizens automatically lost their US citizenship and women could not sponsor their husband's green card.[26] Among other reasons, women were presumed to be naturally subservient to men, aligning their allegiances with their husbands'. But this sort of approach would not be considered acceptable today.)

That said, certain partner migration restrictions affect people from some cultural backgrounds or countries of origin more than others – in a way that policymakers might be perfectly happy with. For example, analysts argue that Denmark's restrictions on partner migration have indirectly aimed to target Muslim couples.[27] This includes a minimum age of 24 years for marriage migration, which has a larger impact on people from communities with conservative religious views, who tend to marry at a younger age. A 'combined attachment' rule until 2019 required couples to have greater attachment to Denmark than any other country, measured by things such as where their family members lived, how long they had lived in Denmark versus other countries, and their language proficiency.[28] This particularly affected ethnic minority Danes marrying someone from their parents' country of origin.

In countries that have signed up to legal frameworks such as the ECHR, policymakers' ability to restrict family life is constrained. For example, a UK attempt to prevent marriage migration for under-21s was struck down in the courts on the basis it violated the ECHR right to family life. Denmark's 'combined attachment' rule was also abolished after a court ruling in 2019 (on this occasion because it violated an association agreement with Turkey, not the ECHR).

The ECHR also has a big impact on individual cases, as it requires governments to assess whether there would be 'unjustifiably harsh' consequences for families. In the UK, the government makes tens of thousands of grants of status every year under the 'family life' route that is designed to ensure compliance with the human rights convention.[29]

Parents and other family members

Most of the discussion so far has been about partners. Governments generally agree to admit partners, albeit sometimes reluctantly. Rules on other relatives, such as elderly parents, are often more restrictive.

In some respects, many of the same arguments that apply to partners also apply to elderly parents. That is, policymakers face a trade-off between the value of allowing family life and the potential costs of supporting family members they bring in. The benefits to families are clear. Citizens with elderly parents abroad gain the ability to care for their parents at home, and are not required to leave the country to do so.

On the other hand, if you were worried about the possible financial costs of partner migration, the economics of parent migration look a lot worse. Retired people no longer pay income tax and often make heavy use of publicly funded healthcare. They may provide some childcare, allowing their working-age children to work more hours. But realistically this is unlikely to offset their fiscal costs, unless they are really quite wealthy. One calculation from the UK suggests that people cost the state between £250,000 and £380,000 between the ages of 80 and 90.[30]

Another difference between parent and partner migration is that if you need a visa for your parents, you probably previously migrated yourself. That's because people who were born citizens of the country they live in are usually going to have parents who are already citizens too. For some, this point will be irrelevant: once someone has become a citizen, they should be treated equally. However, if policymakers knew that a person who arrived on, say, a work visa might later bring their elderly parents to the country, it might have changed the original calculus about whether it was economically beneficial to admit them.

These calculations may seem rather cold-hearted. But if you agree that economics has a role in at least some types of migration decisions – and clearly in the case of work visa holders, it does – the costs of parents cannot be entirely ignored.

Some countries have liberal policies towards parent migration nonetheless. For example, the US allows citizens to sponsor their parents for green cards with no numerical limit or language requirements. Other countries are more restrictive. Australia's approach has been to make applicants pay for the cost of bringing their parents, for example. Its Contributory Parent visa cost around AU$48,500 in 2024, and the person sponsoring their parent also had to agree to repay up to AU$10,000 of any benefits the parent may claim. Compared to the potential costs of parental migration, these figures are not wildly high.

Many people are willing to accept the deal Australia is offering. The small, capped visa category has been heavily oversubscribed and had an estimated 14-year wait as of late 2024.[31] This might seem harsh, but many people will prefer it to the alternative many countries adopt, which is not to allow parents at all – or only when there is a particularly compelling case, such as a parent requiring care that is simply not available in their country of origin.

What is family migration policy for?

Governments find family migration inconvenient. Migration into *low-income* families will usually have an economic cost. Policymakers sometimes also want to restrict family migrants whom they consider to be culturally different from the majority population.

If policymakers in high-income countries could wave a magic wand and find that their residents stopped wanting to marry non-citizens, quite a few would probably take it up. In this hypothetical world, citizens would avoid getting into relationships with people who might not qualify for a visa. Perhaps they would look up visa policy details before they went on a first date, and reject advances from anyone with the wrong immigration status. Policymakers would no longer be faced with the suffering that can ensue when people are separated from their partners – and particularly when one parent is separated from their children.

Since this is not the world we live in, all high-income countries in practice recognize a right to family life. They also impose some restrictions, such as financial requirements and language tests. When deciding how high these barriers should be, the basic dilemma remains: to what extent governments will accept family migration as it comes, or accept the human cost of separating the families they would like to exclude.

6
UNAUTHORIZED MIGRATION AND ENFORCEMENT

Kai came to the UK on a tourist visa but overstayed, working without permission for several years in the hospitality sector. He met a British woman and they had two children. A few years later, they separated, but he continued to play a role in the children's lives, occasionally collecting them from school when their mother was not available. After refusing his application for a residence permit, the immigration enforcement agency started preparing to deport him. Was this the right decision?

This is a fictional but fairly typical example if you read case reports from litigation on residence rights. On one hand, Kai is living in the country without permission, working in low-wage jobs that do not qualify for work visas. He is no longer with his partner, so he doesn't qualify for a partner visa. The government wants to remove him from the country to ensure compliance with the immigration rules – and perhaps to reinforce the principle that unauthorized migrants will not be able to stay.

On the other hand, he has British children, who benefit from his presence. Do their interests trump the interests of the state in removing him? And if so, how close does his relationship with the children have to be to justify not removing him? Do his work and income matter, or is economics irrelevant? What other factors should affect the case – such as whether he is considered a pillar of the local community or has a criminal record?

Cases like these illustrate the conflicts policymakers face when dealing with breaches of immigration law. The complicated web of policies this book has described so far exists because policymakers – quite reasonably – believe that most people will follow them. When they don't, policymakers face conflicts between their interest in enforcing rules they introduced for a reason, and the rights of unauthorized migrants, some of whom may have lived in the country for a while and become part of communities there. In addition, actually removing people with no residence rights is more difficult than it sounds. It is logistically difficult. Human rights law significantly constrains governments attempting to remove people from their territory, although sceptics and liberals disagree about whether unauthorized migrants receive too many or too few legal protections.

What is unauthorized migration?

When you think about unauthorized migration, what comes to mind? For many, the answer will be the most visible examples, such as people crossing the Mediterranean or English Channel by boat. However, many unauthorized migrants arrive legally on tourist visas or other short-term permits, and overstay. A smaller number are born into unauthorized status, if their parents are living in the country without permission. (Most high-income countries do not have birthright citizenship – the US and Canada are unusual in this respect.)[1]

Unauthorized residence happens for various reasons. Most importantly, there is a gap between the supply and demand for legal migration opportunities. Governments want to restrict migration, for all the reasons this book has discussed. If people are sufficiently motivated to move and cannot find a legal option, they may choose unauthorized ones. Some move for work; others move to join their family. Unauthorized entry is one of the main ways refugees access the asylum system in high-income countries, as we will see in the next chapter.

Historically, migration in today's high-income countries was less closely regulated. Even as immigration controls started to develop throughout the 20th century, many countries lacked the funds or administrative capacity for any meaningful enforcement. Enforcing immigration rules is resource-intensive, after all. Many developing countries continue to have lower administrative capacity for either

> **Box 6.1: Illegal? Irregular? Unauthorized? Undocumented?**
>
> The terminology used to describe people moving or living without permission is contested. Academics tend to say 'irregular' migration or migrant, while 'illegal' is more common in public debate. Both mean the same thing but have different connotations. A recent qualitative study (in which I was involved) found that people considered the term 'unauthorized' most impartial.[2] That is the term I use most often, because it is both clear and accurate. I do not use the term 'undocumented' because it can be misleading. Legally resident migrants may lack documentation to prove their status.

implementing immigration rules or enforcing them, and migrating without status is considered much more normal. Globally, much human migration still takes place outside of formal policy regimes. But by the 21st century, all high-income countries had at least some policies designed to prevent people from entering or residing without permission.

How much of a problem is it?

Unauthorized residence is a problem, regardless of your political perspective. First, unauthorized migration makes it harder for governments to implement the immigration and labour laws they want. For example, perhaps policymakers decided to restrict migration into low-wage jobs because they wanted to restrict the growth of low-paid, labour-intensive industries. Employers who recruit workers without legal status undermine that objective. Employing unauthorized residents may also enable companies to violate *other* labour laws such as minimum wages more easily, because workers put up less resistance. In addition, if people arrive without permission, they do not undergo the same security and background checks that immigration agencies conduct when they issue visas.

Second, lacking legal status is bad for migrants themselves. Unauthorized migrants will generally have no right to work, which limits them to a narrow set of jobs where employers are willing to turn a blind eye to their status. They typically lack access to the social safety net and the fear of deportation makes many fearful of seeking help. For example, victims of domestic abuse and other crimes are often reluctant to contact the police – which is why some countries, like the US, offer a dedicated visa for victims of criminal activity. Exploitative employers can threaten their staff with deportation if they don't accept poor conditions. While not all unauthorized migrants experience these problems, evidence of the risks and difficulties they face is widespread.[3]

The vulnerability of unauthorized migrants creates knock-on challenges for government agencies. For example, local governments may need to support destitute families who would otherwise be homeless.

The police may find it harder to do their work if some residents fear contacting them.

Third, unauthorized migration is extremely unpopular. This is partly because of the practical problems I have just outlined, but for many people it is also a matter of principle – a desire to see everyone playing by the rules and government agencies enforcing them.

As a result, unauthorized migration creates a conflict between two objectives. On one hand, governments want to set and enforce immigration and labour laws they believe will protect the interests of their citizens – and that citizens trust are effective. On the other hand, they want to reduce the most serious risks to unauthorized migrants themselves. It is possible to feel real sympathy for people without legal status while also believing that immigration rules are legitimate and should be enforced both for practical reasons and as a matter of principle. The challenge for policymakers is how to balance these aims.

Policies to address unauthorized migration fall into two main categories: giving people legal status or forcing them to leave. In practice, there is also a third strategy that policymakers adopt more quietly alongside the other two: tolerating the presence of unauthorized residents, while restricting their rights. This chapter discusses whether and when these options help policymakers achieve their objectives.

Box 6.2: Whose fault is it? Narratives about unauthorized migration

Debates about enforcement and legalization often make assumptions about who is to blame: policymakers or unauthorized migrants.

Integrity: One narrative prioritizes the integrity of the immigration system. Migrants are presented as rule-breakers who had a responsibility to comply with the immigration rules. The state's job is to enforce those rules in the interests of citizens.

Humanitarian framing: A competing narrative is that the rigid immigration rules *produce* unauthorized status. Migrants are presented as innocent victims of an overly restrictive system that fails to offer enough routes to legal status.

Public debates often present the issue as black and white, relying exclusively on one of these two frames. In reality, elements of both may be true. It is difficult to imagine a functioning immigration system without some enforcement. At the same time, unauthorized migrants are clearly vulnerable to many forms of exploitation.

Enforcement

Debates about immigration enforcement often focus on borders – probably because they are easy for us to imagine. Photos of people scaling fences or boarding small boats symbolize the challenge of immigration control.

It is true that a lot of enforcement activity takes place at physical borders. Between official crossing points, governments often monitor their borders using military-style equipment such as drones, underground movement sensors and thermal imaging. One challenge governments face is that as they ramp up enforcement activity, smugglers look for new weak points. Enforcement then diverts people to less heavily enforced border areas. Analysts compare it to squeezing a balloon.

For example, in the 1990s, the US poured increasing sums into policing the US–Mexico border in urban areas where most illegal crossings took place. As a result, people started crossing in more remote desert areas, where extreme heat and cold made transit more dangerous. Migrants became more reliant on professional smugglers ('coyotes'), and the trips became more expensive. This doesn't mean enforcement has no effect. In the US–Mexico example, it does appear to have reduced the total number of border crossings, but not as much as policymakers had hoped.[4]

However, a lot of immigration enforcement takes place away from the physical border. Over the past few decades many high-income countries have co-opted airlines to conduct visa checks even before

> **Box 6.3: Deaths at the border**
>
> Crossing borders illegally can be dangerous. Every year, the International Organization for Migration verifies thousands of deaths of people attempting to cross borders, and many more go unrecorded. Just over half of people whose deaths they recorded in the decade to 2023 drowned, most in the Mediterranean. Others died in accidents due to hazardous transport (such as suffocating in lorries), or in harsh environmental conditions like desert heat or cold.

passengers board a plane in their direction. Some fund neighbouring countries to prevent potential unauthorized migrants from reaching their borders. And a lot of enforcement activity takes places within the country, after unauthorized migrants arrive.

Interior enforcement and 'hostile environments'

The term 'hostile environment' gained currency in the UK under Home Secretary – and later, Prime Minister – Theresa May, who said that the UK would create a 'really hostile environment' for unauthorized migrants. The idea was to make it difficult for people without legal status to live a normal life, so that they would leave of their own accord.

Variants of the hostile environment policy have existed for decades in high-income countries, however, and include restrictions on access to work, housing, healthcare, benefits or banking. These measures are also known as 'interior enforcement'.

By far the most common measure is fines for employers hiring unauthorized migrants. The European Union (EU) requires all Member States to make it illegal for employers to hire unauthorized migrants, and sets out common sanctions for employers caught violating the rules. There is evidence that employer sanctions work: that is, they discourage at least some employers from employing people without work rights.[5] The stress of living without legal status and the difficulties migrants have accessing work and public services encourages some people to return home.[6]

Employer sanctions do not work on all employers, however: many migrants without legal status are still able to find jobs. Governments' enforcement capacity is often limited. Some employers are willing to turn a blind eye to their workers' immigration status, or do not know how to conduct the checks correctly (for example, accepting the wrong documents).[7] Some deliberately exploit workers' fear of removal, threatening to report them to the immigration authorities if they try to assert their employment rights. As a result, policymakers face a trade-off between the goal of making unauthorized residence unattractive and the risk of increasing exploitation.

Hostile-environment policies may have other unintended consequences. In particular, authorized residents can be caught in the net if they cannot prove their legal status. This is a risk in countries with poor record keeping. The UK's 'Windrush scandal' in 2018 is a prominent example. Legally resident, often elderly, residents who had come legally to the UK decades earlier but had never received residence paperwork were later denied employment, benefits or healthcare as a result of measures designed to target unauthorized migrants. Some were even detained and deported. After the Windrush scandal, the term 'hostile environment' became embarrassing to the UK government, which replaced it with 'compliant environment'. But 'hostile' was more evocative, and the term stuck.

Both border enforcement and interior enforcement make it harder for people to cross borders without permission and live a normal life without legal status. But these measures have their limits. Unless states close their borders, North Korea style, they will still face the challenge of unauthorized populations. Some people will manage to cross without permission, and others will arrive legally and overstay their visas despite attempts to deter them.

It is difficult to measure the size of unauthorized populations that result, although the US has the largest of high-income countries, at an estimated 11 million in 2022.[8] Estimates for Europe are a bit lower, with one study suggesting between 2.6 and 3.2 million migrants were living without authorization in 12 Western and Southern European countries between 2016 and 2023 – with the largest numbers in the UK and Germany.[9] All the estimates need to be taken with a grain of salt, as the true figures simply are not known.

Once people are already living in the country without permission, policymakers who want to tackle this problem have two main options: deportation and legalization.

Deportation

Banishment of citizens and expulsions of foreigners have occurred for millennia, from ostracism in ancient Greece to expulsions of mercenaries, merchants or revolutionaries in 16th- to 19th-century Europe. However, for most of history there were either no nation states or no comprehensive systems of residence rights within nation states, and so no processes for enforcing them.

Today, high-income countries send people back to their countries of citizenship on a relatively large scale. But often policymakers deport fewer people than they would like. That is because removing people is easier said than done.

To understand this challenge, it is useful to consider the perspective of people who are liable for removal. Some are willing to leave if they have to. Perhaps they come from reasonably functional countries where they can envisage building a normal life. Perhaps they never intended to live in the destination country forever anyway. Immigration lawyer Colin Yeo calls such people 'low-resistance' deportees, because they are most likely to cooperate with removal.

Other people liable for removal *really* do not want to leave. For example, perhaps they come from a poorly functioning country where they will face poverty and insecurity. Perhaps they have lived in the destination country for a long time, or have children who do not speak the language of the origin country.

People who do not want to be removed may resist in different ways. Some physically resist. Deportation may sound clinical and straightforward, but forcing people onto planes can be a brutal process.[10] Removals now often involve escorts trained in the use of restraint techniques, typically outnumbering the deportees themselves, as well as medical staff and interpreters.[11]

Crucially, many people liable for removal challenge it the courts. For example, human rights laws sometimes enable people with close family ties to gain legal status. Others raise asylum claims, or challenge removal on medical grounds (for example, if they are receiving medical treatment that could not continue in their country of origin).

Indeed, human rights law and other legal protections have played a significant role in immigration policy in recent decades, particularly in Western European countries that offer more legal protections than others, such as Australia or South Korea. Deportation is one of the areas where the role of human rights law is clearest.[12] These rights are hotly contested. They are designed to protect individuals from abuses by the state. In immigration policy this often means restricting governments' ability to detain and deport non-citizens. Processing legal claims also takes time and resources. Even unsuccessful challenges delay removals while they are being heard. When bureaucracies are inefficient – due to under-resourced immigration agencies, courts or legal aid systems – it can it take months or even years to look at the legal claims. Analysts disagree on whether human rights law has got the balance right between the interests of states and individuals' rights.

A final barrier to removing people without residence rights is that the country they come from must agree to take them back. Countries are obliged to take back their citizens under international law, but can put up many barriers in practice. For example, people liable for removal often destroy their identity documents. The country of origin might then refuse to provide travel documents (perhaps denying that the person in question is their citizen) or do it so slowly that it disrupts the deportation process.

All these barriers make returning unauthorized migrants difficult and expensive. The practical challenges are much lower if people are willing to cooperate with their removal. Many countries run 'voluntary returns' programmes – though the word 'voluntary' here is obviously a bit euphemistic. These programmes often give financial incentives to encourage people to return home; for example, the UK offered up to £3,000 as of 2025. Despite the payment, voluntary returns are still cheaper than deportation. They are also less likely to involve force or periods of immigration detention. However, they will not be feasible in all cases, most notably those where the people being removed fight hardest against it.

Legalization

Legalizations – also known as amnesties or regularizations – are controversial. Critics argue that it is wrong to reward rule-breaking by giving people status if they arrived illegally or overstayed a visa. By definition, legalization typically involves giving legal status to people who are not otherwise eligible for status under the normal immigration system – that is, as workers, family members or refugees.

Supporters of legalization tend to emphasize humanitarian arguments. For example, having legal status makes people less vulnerable to exploitation and may enable them to participate more fully in society. It may improve migrants' economic prospects, since they are no longer confined to the lowest-paying jobs,[13] and their employers have less control over them.[14] Some studies even suggest that legalizations make migrants less likely to commit property crimes, by increasing their options in the regular labour market.[15]

Some advocates of legalization also argue that it brings wider economic benefits. Legalized workers are more likely to work on the books and in better jobs – paying more tax. However, in the medium run they will also become eligible for benefits. Studies have come to different conclusions on whether the net effect on public finances is positive or negative.[16] Either way, the impact on public finances appears to be relatively small and so is not the major reason for considering or rejecting the legalization policy option.

Does legalization encourage more unauthorized migration?

A common criticism of legalization is that it will encourage more people to migrate without permission. One-off amnesties usually aim to address this concern by using a cut-off date. People can only qualify if they were already living in the country before that date. However, some countries have conducted repeated legalizations – such as Spain and Italy in the 1990s and 2000s. If people do not believe the amnesty is really 'one off', they might be more willing to migrate without permission in hope of another one. After all, there is evidence that the ability to secure legal status makes migration considerably more attractive.[17]

In practice, it is very difficult to measure whether the pull factor is real, because data on unauthorized migration is – almost by definition – extremely limited. One study looked at detected attempts to cross the US–Mexico border before and after the US 1986 Immigration Reform and Control Act, a landmark piece of legislation that gave legal status to around 2.7 million people. It found that the amnesty did not change long-term illegal migration patterns from Mexico.[18] European studies have mostly found similar results. An exception is a 2014 study that found more unauthorized migrants were detected in EU countries that had conducted an amnesty in the past,[19] albeit using low-quality data. Overall, the evidence is arguably not strong enough to draw firm conclusions.

Regardless of whether one-off legalizations *encourage* more people to migrate in future, there are other reasons they are unlikely to fix the problem of unauthorized populations for the long term. In particular, the push and pull factors that encouraged unauthorized migration often remain in place, such as strong employer demand for low-wage workers. After its 1986 legalization, the US poured progressively greater resources into border control and interior enforcement. This did not stop the unauthorized population growing to an estimated 8.6 million by 2000 (only 14 years later) and remaining stubbornly high thereafter.[20]

In other words, policymakers considering legalization need to be realistic. The policy may well help reduce *current* migrants' vulnerability to exploitation or poverty, but cannot wipe the slate clean in the long term.

Perhaps as a result, some countries have smaller, ongoing policies that allow some unauthorized residents to gain legal status case by case. For example, the UK and many EU countries allow people to apply for legal status on human rights grounds (see Box 6.4). The evidence on whether these programmes affect prospective migrants' decision-making is virtually non-existent.

Legal migration routes

Should states offer more legal migration pathways instead of waiting for people to become unauthorized migrants and then legalizing them? Many advocates on the liberal side of the debate – and particularly in business – have suggested that offering work visas

Box 6.4: Human rights applications for legal status in the UK

The UK sets out detailed criteria for regularization based on the 'right to private or family life', which derives from the European Convention on Human Rights (ECHR). The rules allow some people without residence rights to remain in the country.

Applicants can apply based on a relationship with a British or long-term resident child if they have a sufficiently meaningful role in their upbringing. Others can apply based on long residence: for example, an adult can qualify if they have lived in the UK for at least 20 years. The required residence is shorter for children who have spent most of their lives in the UK.

Other adults can make the case that there would be very significant obstacles to re-integrating in their country of citizenship or to taking their partner with them. For example, in one illustrative case, an appeal judge eventually ruled in favour of a Pakistani man who had overstayed a student visa and made multiple claims on asylum and human rights grounds over the course of a decade, all of which were refused. He was eventually allowed to stay on the grounds that his 51-year-old British partner, who had no prior connection with Pakistan, could not speak Urdu, would be unlikely to be able to continue her work as a teacher in Pakistan, and would have no social support network.[21]

for low-wage work could help reduce unauthorized migration. After all, the lack of legal work opportunities is one of the factors driving the phenomenon.

In practice, it seems relatively unlikely that expanding low-wage work visa programmes would significantly reduce unauthorized migration – although the evidence is too limited to draw confident conclusions.[22] There are two main reasons. First, legal labour migration routes would have to be large and liberal enough to provide a realistic alternative to unauthorized working. Low-wage labour programmes are often heavily regulated, because governments want to ensure migrant workers are not exploited. In the US, even a relatively large agricultural visa programme has not prevented employers from relying on unauthorized workers. Crucially, states have their reasons for restricting migration into low-wage jobs. They may be reluctant to offer sufficiently large programmes to make a difference.

Second, expanding legal migration today could make unauthorized migration in future years more likely, by increasing the size of migrant communities and so making the country more attractive to future migrants. For example, post-war 'guestworker' programmes in the US and Europe are one of several factors that contributed to establishing migrant populations there. The resulting social networks and family ties were important drivers of both authorized and unauthorized migration after that.

But ultimately, the impact of legal channels on unauthorized work-related immigration is an empirical question and the jury is still out.

What is policy on unauthorized migration for?

If you support the idea of having border controls, some enforcement is inevitable. Border enforcement, checks on people's status within the country, and deportations all aim to achieve policymakers' main objective of admitting or retaining only those migrants they consider beneficial.

The enforcement process itself brings new challenges for governments, however. Perhaps the most important tension is between the desire to uphold the law and the desire or legal obligation to treat migrants with humanity. Enforcement can be a brutal process with harsh consequences for the people concerned. Policymakers need to decide how severe the consequences are that they are willing to impose, and what is proportionate to achieve their aims.

This tension between the integrity of the system and respect for the individual also plays out in public opinion. On one hand, unauthorized migration is unpopular: publics want to see immigration rules enforced. At the same time, voters are often amenable to legalization if they find the people to be regularized sufficiently sympathetic. For example, a 2024 US poll found that a majority supported 'mass deportations', but a similar majority also supported legalizing unauthorized migrants who were married to

US citizens.[23] A study in Austria, Italy, Poland, Sweden and the UK found greater support for legalization when applicants were described as workers with a history of employment.[24]

The question of how to balance the rights of individuals versus the integrity of the immigration system becomes even more difficult to resolve when the migrants are refugees. The next chapter turns to that question.

7
REFUGEES AND ASYLUM SEEKERS

Take the example of someone who enters our country illegally on a small boat. Travelling through multiple safe EU countries. France, Italy, Spain. Shopping around for where they claim asylum. Making that final and extremely dangerous Channel crossing to the United Kingdom, while lining the pockets of despicable international criminal gangs. Our broken system is enabling this international criminal trade. It is disregarding the most vulnerable, elbowing women and children in need to the side. Trampling over the weak. That cannot be right. (Priti Patel, UK Home Secretary, 4 October 2020)

We need to bring an end to men, women and children who have fled war and oppression in countries such as Afghanistan, Syria and Iran being driven into the arms of the smuggling gangs, by opening safe routes so refugees wanting to be with their families are not forced to take deadly risks. (Enver Solomon, Refugee Council, 14 July 2024)

These quotes show two very different ways of framing the same phenomenon: people crossing the Channel from France to the UK without permission, to claim asylum.

Despite their differences, the speakers appear to agree on two points. First, people genuinely in need of protection should receive it *somewhere*. Second, they should not be making dangerous, unauthorized journeys.

They disagree on the solution. Migration liberals argue for safe routes that would enable people to receive asylum without first violating immigration law and say that high-income countries have a responsibility to accept refugees from the world's conflict zones even if they are not neighbouring countries. Migration sceptics criticize the asylum system for offering migrants a 'trump card' that allows them to bypass the normal immigration rules.[1] They argue refugees should stay in safe countries closer to their country of origin, rather than travelling on to high-income countries that offer better economic opportunities.

Here, in microcosm, is the debate about the global protection system. Nobody thinks the current system works very well. But agreeing on a solution is no easy task. This chapter explores why.

How did we get here?

The current global protection regime for refugees dates back to the 1951 Refugee Convention. Reeling from the shock of the Holocaust and the forced displacement of millions of Europeans, a group of mostly European countries negotiated an agreement that committed them to protecting refugees who had arrived on their territory. Unlike Jewish refugees who had attempted to flee genocidal regimes in Europe and were turned away,[2] refugees in future would have the right to a hearing and to protection if they qualified for it.

The Refugee Convention defines a refugee as a person with 'a well-founded fear of being persecuted for reasons of race, religion, nationality, membership of a particular social group or political opinion, is outside the country of his nationality and is unable or, owing to such fear, is unwilling to avail himself of the protection of that country'.

The 1951 Convention initially only applied to people displaced in Europe by the Second World War and was conceived of as temporary. However, a further Protocol extended it in 1967 to cover all refugees, making the arrangement permanent.* Today, people granted asylum in high-income countries come from all across the world. In the European Union (EU), for example, the top countries of origin for people granted asylum in 2024 were Afghanistan, Syria, Eritrea, Palestine, Turkey, Somalia, Iran and Iraq.[3]

---

* In this chapter I use the term 'Refugee Convention' to refer to both the Convention and the Protocol.

Other legal agreements also affect how asylum seekers and refugees are treated. The 1984 Convention Against Torture and the European Convention on Human Rights (ECHR) prohibit states from returning people to places where they could be tortured, regardless of whether they qualify for protection as a refugee. For example, people who have been convicted of serious crimes are excluded from refugee status under the Refugee Convention, but cannot be deported if there is a real risk they could be tortured on return.

While some major refugee-hosting states, such as Jordan, Pakistan and Indonesia, are not signatories to the Refugee Convention, a majority of states worldwide (149 in total) had signed either the Convention or its 1967 Protocol by 2025. The Convention Against Torture has been ratified by 175 states. Let's look in more detail at how the rules work in practice.

The most important obligation in the Refugee Convention is the idea of *non-refoulement*, which means 'not pushing back'. Signatories agree not to send refugees to places where they could be at risk of persecution.

Refugees only receive these rights once they arrive on a country's territory. The Convention does not oblige states to provide safe routes for people to reach their territory, nor does it explicitly require refugees to arrive legally or claim in the first safe country they reach. The result is a system predicated on unauthorized journeys.

Indeed, the Convention explicitly provides for this, stating that refugees should not be penalized for their illegal entry or presence if they have 'good cause' for it. Unauthorized journeys are often dangerous too, such as crossing the Mediterranean or the Darién Gap between Colombia and Panama. This makes the day-to-day reality of the asylum system unpopular. It involves dangerous and disorderly journeys that put people at risk and symbolize the state's loss of control.

Another crucial feature of the global asylum system is that it assumes states can sort applicants neatly into 'refugee' and 'non-refugee' boxes (see Box 7.1). Refugees receive protection, while non-refugees can be removed. People who do not qualify as refugees are often referred to as 'economic migrants' – although some may be moving for other reasons, such as to join family.

The fact that asylum applicants include both refugees and non-refugees creates huge operational and ethical difficulties. Policymakers will often want to take a tough approach to deterring people who do not require protection, while dealing more generously with refugees. But when a person applies for asylum, the state does not know who is in which group. As a result, non-refugees receive protections designed to protect refugees (most obviously, protection from removal), while refugees are hit with policies designed for economic migrants (such as limits on the right to work and levels of financial support that put them well below the poverty line).

The longer it takes for governments to complete the asylum process and decide whether or not applicants are refugees, the more problematic this becomes. Being kept out of the labour market while waiting for an

Box 7.1: Deciding who is a refugee

How do governments know who is a refugee and who is not? As you can probably imagine, it is not an easy task. Many people would like to migrate and most will lack the skills, connections and good luck typically required to get a work visa. As a result, they have an incentive to say they are refugees. Some people do not know whether they are refugees or not; after all, the rules are quite complex.

The process of distinguishing between refugees and other migrants is known as a 'refugee status determination'. Applicants must convince a government official that they face a genuine risk of persecution if they return home. Some have documentary evidence such as correspondence or medical reports. Others just their word. Many applicants find the process degrading, and feel that they encounter a 'culture of disbelief' from government officials.[4] Critics argue that officials expect neatly packaged narratives about how the applicant became a refugee, and are suspicious of people who do not fit with the stereotypes of the vulnerable victim.[5] There is less research on whether people with fabricated stories manage to receive asylum, although governments occasionally prosecute unscrupulous immigration lawyers for encouraging the practice.[6]

It is very hard to say how many refugees are refused asylum and how many people receive it even though they do not qualify. What we do know is that different decision-makers come to different conclusions even when they are supposedly applying the same set of laws. In the EU, around half of applicants in 2023 were granted refugee status or another kind of protection at initial decision stage, but it varies a lot by country. For example, Germany granted asylum to 87 percent of Afghan applicants in 2024, while Belgium granted only 39 percent.[7] In the US, some immigration judges decide that most applicants are refugees while others deny asylum to all but a small percentage of cases.[8]

From start to finish, refugee status determination is time-consuming and often expensive. When faced with a large influx of refugees, destination states often do not even attempt the task. For example, developing countries neighbouring conflict zones have typically accepted refugees who cross their borders purely based on their nationality, without attempting to assess each one. Examples include Syrians fleeing to Turkey or Venezuelans in Colombia. And when Russia invaded Ukraine and over four million people fled to the EU,[9] EU policymakers agreed to bypass the asylum system and give Ukrainians temporary protection without any individual assessment. Realistically they had little choice, since their asylum systems would otherwise have been overwhelmed. Policies that carefully distinguish between refugees and other migrants are in some respects the luxury of countries far from the front line.

asylum decision has a long-term negative impact on refugees' wellbeing.[10] At the same time, long delays mean that people who don't qualify for refugee status are not being removed. Some end up staying so long that they become eligible for legal status on different human rights grounds, such as family ties.

Why do refugees move to high-income states?

Most people are displaced in developing countries, where war, conflict and violence are most common. These conflicts are often quite distant from high-income countries. As a result, outbreaks of conflict often mean people flee across just one border to find safety within the region. For example, when conflict broke out in Sudan in 2023, the large majority of the people who fled the country went to neighbouring countries such as Egypt, Ethiopia and South Sudan.[11]

Some people who flee across borders never plan to return. Others prefer to stay close by because they hope to be able to go back home when the situation settles down. The longer the conflict lasts, the less hope they have of return and the more they are likely to look for somewhere to build their life permanently away from home. But this can be difficult in neighbouring countries. Refugees in developing countries such as Bangladesh, Lebanon or Turkey sometimes face legal or bureaucratic barriers to working, restrictions on movement, curfews, or harassment and discrimination.[12] Many of the developing countries that host refugees have little interest in integrating them locally, and are happy to see refugees move on.

As a result, one study argues that the huge difference in living standards between places of first asylum and high-income destinations 'turns refugees into economic migrants', encouraging them to move on to places where their prospects are better.[13] This is despite some high-income countries' efforts to deter onward migration by providing development assistance or asking developing countries to provide legal work rights for refugees.[14]

The Refugee Convention is not the only thing that makes this onward movement possible. For example, many people fleeing the war in Syria went to work in Gulf countries, which don't recognize refugee status but gave them work or visit visas.[15] However, asylum systems work as a safety net for the large numbers of people who cannot find other legal visas.

> **Box 7.2: Does the asylum system favour the least vulnerable?**
>
> A common criticism of the current global asylum regime is that its reliance on clandestine journeys makes it harder for the poorest and most vulnerable refugees to access protection.
>
> For example, one consequence is that people who make longer journeys to reach high-income countries are more likely to be men, because men are more willing to accept risks.[16] According to the United Nations (UN), around half of people displaced worldwide are female.[17] But asylum applicants in high-income countries are much more likely to be men. The gender balance evens out slightly once you

take into account family reunion: that is, men often travel first and then apply to bring female family members through a safer route once they have received asylum. Nonetheless, male refugees remain more likely to access protection in high-income countries, even after taking into account family reunion.

A competing protection system exists that does not require people to have the resources and risk tolerance for dangerous journeys. This system, known as refugee resettlement, is run by the UN refugee agency, UNHCR. The UN identifies displaced people whom they consider particularly in need of resettlement. Host countries then take an agreed number of people. Destination states can also pick and choose, and they do. Often, they choose women and families; sometimes, they select people they consider particularly vulnerable (for example, due to medical needs). But this system is voluntary and small. Large Western European countries typically voluntarily resettle up to a couple of thousand refugees per year, but grant thousands or tens of thousands of people refugee status through their asylum systems.[18]

Box 7.3: Are climate migrants refugees?

Climate change is likely to affect migration patterns in coming decades, although precisely how much is disputed. Drought, natural disasters, declines in fishing stocks or conflicts exacerbated by competition for resources can be

> consequences of changes in climate and can also create 'push factors' for migration. It is not always clear which of these problems has been created or worsened by climate change. And even if it was, it would often still be hard to classify any particular person as a 'climate migrant'.
>
> People who leave regions affected by changes in their natural environment will often be doing so primarily for economic reasons. They would not count as refugees under current international law even if they must move to survive – unless the changes in climate had fuelled conflicts that led to specific social groups being persecuted. Some states may accept climate migrants following natural disasters, but international refugee law does not oblige them to.

Why many policymakers dislike the asylum system

Governments have signed the Refugee Convention and for the most part they want to be seen to comply. The basic idea of *non-refoulement* has a lot of support. Few commentators argue that countries ought to send people back to countries if they are genuinely at risk of serious harm there.

In practice, though, policymakers in high-income countries often do not really want to accept many people through their asylum systems, for three main reasons.

First, the asylum system gives policymakers very little control. Governments have a basic interest in maintaining orderly and controlled borders, minimizing unauthorized entries. Such arrivals reduce governments' ability to conduct background checks.

Governments also like to pick and choose their refugees, while keeping the numbers small and predictable – but this approach is incompatible with the Refugee Convention.

Evidence from Europe suggests that members of the public tend to support numerical limits on asylum.[19] They may also prefer to welcome refugees from particular conflicts or with particular characteristics, such as women and children. Indeed, some scholars have argued that the main reason high-income countries have ramped up enforcement policies to prevent asylum seekers from arriving over the last few decades was that – unlike when the Refugee Convention was first drafted in Europe – most refugees are no longer White.[20]

In some countries, court decisions expanding countries' obligations towards refugees have contributed to concerns about a loss of control. For example, some types of claims that the drafters of the Refugee Convention did not foresee have now become relatively common, such as claims based on persecution by non-state actors like gangs or perpetrators of domestic violence. Case law in some countries has expanded asylum law to add new forms of protection. For some onlookers, this expansion is a sensible process that keeps the Convention up to date. For others, it is a stealthy policy liberalization conducted without democratic consent.

Second, many countries struggle to remove people who are refused refugee status. In theory, people refused asylum can be sent back home. However, asylum seekers who do not qualify for refugee status present a cost in the short run, as they must be supported and have their claims processed. And in practice, removing people to other countries is an expensive, difficult and sometimes violent task – as I discussed in Chapter 6. Many refused asylum seekers remain in the country and join the unauthorized population and shadow economy.

Third, refugees will often present an economic cost. Of course, there are impressive stories of successful refugees, such as Dutch fashion designer Omar Munie, who fled Somalia as a child, or American venture capitalist Semyon Dukach, a child refugee from the former Soviet Union. Some larger refugee groups have also fared relatively well, such as the Ugandan Asians who fled to the UK in the 1960s and 1970s, or Bosnian refugees heading for Austria and Sweden in the 1990s.[21]

However, refugees in many wealthy countries have low employment rates and require substantial support.[22] Employment rates tend to start low and increase substantially over time, although most studies find that refugees' earnings remain low long term.[23] As a result, refugees will often present a net cost to public finances over the course of their lifetimes – although we should expect the figures to vary a lot by country. With the caveat that all fiscal studies require a lot of speculative assumptions, a Dutch study calculated a lifetime net cost of between €350,000 and €400,000 for refugees arriving in their late twenties.[24] Australia's Treasury calculated the cost at AU$400,000 (around £225,000) in 2018–2019.[25] In Canada, where refugees do better in the labour market, net lifetime costs have been estimated in the high tens of thousands (in 2016 Canadian dollars) for refugees arriving before age 40, excluding the cost of public services.[26] Outcomes for refugees appear to be among the best in the US, where one study found that adult refugees roughly broke even for the government during the first 20 years after arrival, paying US$21,000 more in taxes than they received in benefits, cumulatively over that full period (that is, about US$1,000 per year).[27] However, this calculation did not include the substantial costs that arise when people move into retirement.

In my experience, people who are positive about migration often like to suggest that wealthy countries have a lot to gain economically from admitting refugees. The evidence on refugee employment rates and earnings suggests that this is unlikely. There are other reasons countries might want to admit refugees. Economics is usually not one of them.

Enforcement and deterrence

The upshot is that even if states want to comply with the Refugee Convention for ethical or reputational reasons, they also have an incentive to limit access to asylum in practice. The Refugee Convention does not allow them to impose any numerical limits on asylum after refugees have arrived.

As a result, governments in high-income countries have developed several strategies to prevent or deter potential asylum seekers from reaching their territory.

For example, Australia has long intercepted and turned back boats carrying people claiming asylum. The UK and Canada cancel visa-free travel rights from countries if their nationals start to claim asylum in meaningful numbers. The EU struck deals with Turkey and Libya to police border areas to prevent people from setting off across by sea towards EU countries, and the UK has done the same with France.

Some countries have designated particular areas of their territory as places that 'don't really count' as reaching their territory. A famous example is the US 'wet foot, dry foot' policy, which gave residence rights to Cubans who reached US territory only if they had reached dry land – creating a bizarre series of legal wrangles about whether lighthouses and bridges were truly 'dry'.

These policies have been controversial. Critics argue that high-income states use them to offload their responsibilities towards refugees onto developing countries, which host the lion's share of the world's refugees. Supporters counter that if refugees have already found safety *somewhere*, there is no longer an ethical obligation to offer them refugee status. Resolving this dispute is difficult, because states have not agreed how responsibilities should be shared – a question we will return to later in the chapter.

Legally, many enforcement and deterrence policies are compatible with the Refugee Convention. For example, the Convention does not give refugees the right to choose which country offers them protection, which in theory means that countries can agree among themselves who will look at the claim. The EU's 'Dublin' system effectively does this: EU countries have a set of rules to decide which country takes responsibility for asylum seekers – often the first EU country they arrived in. (At least in theory. The actual process of transferring people within the EU has often been bogged down in bureaucracy.)

Other laws or agreements sometimes restrict states' ability to implement enforcement or deterrence policies. For example, the European Court of Human Rights rulings made it harder for European states to send asylum seekers back to countries they have passed through on their journey, such as Greece and Italy.[28] In 2024, Italy's attempt to send to Albania asylum seekers from countries it deemed safe, such as Egypt and Bangladesh, was initially struck down by an Italian court, relying on earlier European Court of Human Rights decisions.

Beyond ethics, enforcement and deterrence policies provoke two main debates. First, whether the policies are effective. And second, how they affect refugees themselves and the global protection regime.

Do deterrence and enforcement work?

The effects of deterrence and enforcement policies are disputed but appear to depend a lot on geography.

In some scenarios, policymakers have been able to reduce asylum arrivals. For example, Canada saw a sharp decline in the number of Mexican citizens claiming asylum after early 2024, when they imposed a visa requirement on Mexicans that made it much harder to set foot on Canadian soil.[29]

Australia has been able to intercept boats approaching the country without permission because boats travelling such long distances are relatively large and robust. The boats are also travelling through international waters, so Australian ships can intercept them outside of the territorial waters of other countries (notably Indonesia).

Physical enforcement is more difficult in some contexts, however. Long land borders winding through remote areas can be particularly difficult to enforce, as the US has found for many decades. In the maritime context, the UK and France took the position in the early 2020s that intercepting flimsy dinghies in the English Channel without the passengers' cooperation was often too dangerous. Government attempts to 'smash the gangs' do not necessarily work: as long as there is money to be made in the smuggling business, new people often step in to replace gang members who have been taken down.

Physical enforcement also does not prevent people on visas from applying for asylum. Australia may have prevented asylum seekers from arriving by boat, but in 2024 still received approaching 25,000 asylum applications from 'airplane people' who had arrived with valid visas.

Because physical enforcement is not always possible, many countries have also tried to deter asylum seekers by making their asylum systems less attractive. Policies have ranged from restricting benefits payments for people with pending asylum claims to sending asylum seekers to other countries. There is some evidence that deterrence policies like these have some impact at the margins, but often not as much as policymakers hope.[30]

Why? While some asylum seekers know quite a lot about asylum policies, others know next to nothing. Some are quite shocked to discover the deterrence policies that await them after they arrive. Perhaps more importantly, even well-informed prospective migrants are often willing to tolerate the discomforts and risks policymakers hope will discourage them.[31] One study of prospective migrants in Senegal found that the average prospective unauthorized migrant was willing to accept a risk of death as high as 25 percent in order to migrate.[32] Migrants often *overestimate* the risks of dying on their journey, but decide to travel nonetheless.[33]

One policy that should in theory have a deterrent effect is preventing all asylum seekers from ever settling at their destination. Research with prospective migrants suggests that the option to get legal status at the end of the process is an important factor.[34] Australia was able to deter people from arriving on small boats through a combination of physical enforcement and a ban on settling in the country as a refugee (see Box 7.4).

The now defunct UK–Rwanda deal purported to do the same. Under the deal, some asylum seekers would have been sent to Rwanda and, if their claim was recognized, they would have received refugee status in Rwanda and never return to the UK. However, the likely deterrent effect was hard to predict because the government was cagey about whether a meaningful share of asylum seekers would have gone to Rwanda in practice. If the numbers were small, it is more likely that asylum seekers would see the programme as simply one more risk at the end of an already risky journey.

> **Box 7.4: Australia's 'Pacific Solution'**
>
> In 2013, Australia announced that all asylum seekers arriving by boat without permission would become ineligible to settle in Australia (people arriving by plane continued to face the normal asylum rules). Their asylum cases would be processed 'offshore' in either Nauru or Papua New Guinea and refugees would be sent to other countries to settle there instead. There were no exceptions. Children, pregnant women – everyone was sent offshore.
>
> At the same time, Australia intercepted boats heading towards its territory and turned them back to neighbouring countries. The policy relied on cooperation from Indonesia, which turned a blind eye to the boat turnbacks.
>
> Together, the measures appear to have dramatically reduced unauthorized boat arrivals, although it is not clear how much of the decline results from deterrence

> versus physical enforcement. Analysts argue that the boat turnbacks were primarily responsible, though it is difficult to prove conclusively.[35]
>
> The policy was also controversial. Critics pointed to poor living conditions, prolonged detention of adults and children, and the high financial costs of operating asylum processing in remote locations. Recognized refugees were left in limbo for long periods, because it took years for the Australian government to find other countries who would agree to accept them. A decade after the policy first begun, a third of the people who had been transferred offshore – about 1,000 people – were in Australia on a temporary basis because the government had not been able to find anywhere for them to go.[36]

The main drawback of enforcement and deterrence policies is the human cost. The Australian example illustrates this challenge: deterrence policies will only work if they make unauthorized journeys significantly less appealing – but achieving this often involves serious hardships for migrants and refugees. That can include long periods of prison-like conditions of immigration detention.

These human costs are most visible in cases where deterrence policies fail to deter. In many policymakers' ideal world, they would threaten harsh consequences for people who arrive unauthorized to claim asylum, but never have to impose these consequences on real people. In the real world, not everyone will get the message about the harsh consequences and some will

WHAT IS IMMIGRATION POLICY FOR?

Figure 7.1: Pro-refugee protesters outside Balmain town hall where an Australian Labor Party caucus meeting was being held

still be willing to take the risk. As a result, people who support the goal of cracking down on asylum in a high-income destination might nonetheless be uncomfortable about the reality of the policies involved.

Safe routes

A different strategy to discourage people from making dangerous or illegal journeys to claim asylum is to offer legal routes instead. Quotas for legal routes tend to be small and their eligibility criteria exclude most prospective asylum seekers.

The traditional 'safe route' for refugees is resettlement through the UN, as described earlier. Resettlement programmes enable people who have already been identified as refugees to settle legally and permanently in another country. Destination countries can specify their preferences. For example, many prefer to resettle women, children or families, rather than single men.[37] One scholar argues that governments choosing refugees are interested in 'promising victims': people who are vulnerable *now*, but who will not have too much trouble becoming economically self-sufficient and blending in culturally in the future.[38]

Other legal routes exist outside of the UN system. For example, after the fall of Kabul to the Taliban in 2021, countries including the US and UK set up resettlement schemes for Afghans who were at risk because they had helped their military intervention there (for example, as interpreters). Indeed, high-income countries are often most willing to set up bespoke protection schemes for people fleeing their geopolitical enemies. Examples include US programmes to accept people fleeing communist regimes in Cuba and China during the Cold War and, more recently, UK and US schemes for Ukrainians escaping the full-scale Russian invasion in 2022.

Some countries offer work visas specifically targeted at people with skills who also qualify as refugees. For example, the non-profit organization Talent Beyond Boundaries has worked with governments in high-income European and English-speaking countries to set up programmes that match recognized refugees to jobs that qualify for work permits. Others, such as Canada, run 'community sponsorship' schemes that allow local community groups to sponsor refugees to be resettled and commit to providing them with financial and other support. Both these schemes are likely to reduce the costs of supporting refugees, by admitting people who will have non-state sources of employment or support.

These schemes are very different but they have something in common which distinguishes them from the ordinary asylum system. They all allow selection. States want to be able to discriminate between different groups of refugees, identifying people they consider most needy or best able to fit in to their societies – or in some cases, people to whom they feel they owe a particular responsibility.

Do 'safe and legal' routes reduce unauthorized migration?

Protecting refugees outside of the asylum system clearly enables governments to admit people in an orderly fashion. Less clear is how much safe routes help *prevent* the use of dangerous ones.

On one hand, the safety and legality of the migration routes are among the most important factors in prospective migrants' decision-making.[39] Unsurprisingly, migrants themselves are keen to use safe, legal routes where they exist. For example, when the UK opened a visa route for Ukrainians fleeing the Russian invasion, over 250,000 people successfully applied.[40] Meanwhile, almost no Ukrainians were detected arriving in the UK illegally. Why would they, when they could simply apply for a visa?

But most safe routes are not like the UK's Ukraine programme, which had no limit on the number of visas.

Most legal routes are small and target specific groups of displaced people. If safe routes have limited numbers and don't cover everyone, people who cannot secure a place may still decide to move without permission.

At the same time as the UK implemented a large visa programme for Ukrainians, it also operated a much smaller resettlement programme for Afghans. But most Afghans who wanted to come to the UK could not secure a place, and Afghans were one of the largest nationalities arriving across the English Channel in small boats.[41]

As a result, safe and legal routes may only have a meaningful impact on illegal journeys if policymakers go big. Realistically, 'safe routes' policies present a trade-off between two common policy objectives: making arrivals more orderly, and accepting fewer

Figure 7.2: The US side of a border wall between the United States and Mexico in Douglas, Southeastern Arizona

refugees. The reality is that the danger and chaos of the journeys is one of the tools destination countries use to keep numbers low.

> **Box 7.5: The United States' experiment with large-scale safe routes**
>
> Unauthorized migration across the US–Mexico border has been a major political issue in the US for decades. For a long time, illegal border crossings had usually involved single men arriving for work and hoping to avoid detection. After 2019, however, this migration took on a new character, with much larger numbers of families fleeing a combination of poverty, gang violence and disorder in Central America and further afield. Instead of taking clandestine routes, people announced themselves at the border and claimed asylum. Many would not qualify as refugees under the Refugee Convention, but an asylum backlog of over two million cases was so large that they could still expect to remain in the US for years while waiting for their case to be heard.
>
> At the beginning of the COVID-19 pandemic, the first Trump administration started to expel large numbers of people who crossed the border without authorization without considering their asylum claims, under a temporary public-health measure known as Title 42. Looking for alternatives ahead of its expiry in May 2023, the Biden administration opened large-scale routes to enter the country lawfully, while restricting asylum for those who did not take them:

- An app, known as CBP One, allowed people to schedule appointments at the Southwest border, where they could claim asylum. Applicants were screened for potential security threats and then admitted to the country while waiting for their asylum case to be heard.
- People from Cuba, Haiti, Nicaragua and Venezuela (known as CHNV) could apply to come legally to the US for up to two years with a status known as 'parole', if they had a US sponsor. Mexico agreed to take back people from the same countries who were removed after crossing without permission.
- Certain people who had not used one of the safe routes and had travelled through another country on their way to the US could be presumed ineligible for asylum.
- Safe Mobility Offices resettled people from Latin America. Unlike traditional UN resettlement, people could apply to be resettled rather than wait to be picked, although the numbers were relatively small.

Demand to migrate under these programmes was enormous. On the first day the CPB One app was open, more than 449,000 users attempted to log in.[42] From January 2023 to December 2024, over 936,000 people successfully scheduled appointments to be admitted using the CBP One app. An additional 532,000 had arrived lawfully through the 'parole' programme for Cubans, Haitians, Nicaraguans and Venezuelans.[43] That adds up to over 730,000 people per year, over the main two years the programmes ran.

The impact of these measures is difficult to discern. Initially the number of people crossing the Southwest border without permission fell after the safe routes were introduced. It proved temporary: detected crossings surged to a record high at the end of 2023 – perhaps driven by people who were unable to secure a place on one of the legal routes or did not know about them. Border patrol agents recorded 1.5 million encounters with people crossing the border unlawfully in the year ending September 2024. A statistical analysis covering late 2011 to mid-2023 found that policies facilitating legal crossings explained only 9 percent of the monthly variation in illegal ones.[44]

It was not until harsher enforcement measures were brought in that the US saw a large and more sustained decline in people detected crossing the border without permission. Mexico stepped up enforcement to stop people reaching the US border in January 2024.[45] In June 2024, the Biden administration further restricted access to asylum for people who had entered without permission, fast-tracking them for removal. By the second half of 2024, unauthorized border crossings had dropped sharply.

Some analysts argue that the enforcement activity would have been less effective if safe routes had not existed: that is, that safe routes and enforcement were complements rather than substitutes.[46] However, detected crossings fell even further when the second Trump administration abruptly *cancelled* the legal routes in January 2025, instead adopting aggressive and highly publicized enforcement operations. At the time of writing, it was too early to say whether the large decline in unauthorized crossings would be sustained.

None of this is conclusive evidence: it's always hard to unpick the effect of each policy against the chaotic backdrop of everything else that affects migration. But overall, it's hard to look at the US experience and conclude that its safe routes were a reliable tool to reduce unauthorized arrivals.

Can high-income countries replace the territorial asylum system?

Many policymakers would like to replace the asylum system with a more orderly system of resettlement or other safe routes. Both migration liberals and sceptics have an interest in reducing unauthorized journeys, even if they disagree on how big the safe routes should be.

Introducing authorized routes is easy – operationally, at least. Removing unauthorized ones is much harder.

In theory, a country that does not mind violating international refugee law can declare that it will not accept some or all refugees who have arrived without permission. The US and UK adopted variants of this approach in the 2024 asylum regulation and 2023 Illegal Migration Act, respectively. (Both were subject to legal challenge.)

But then what? Even if a country is willing to welcome more refugees as part of a programme of safe and legal routes, it still needs a plan to deal with

Figure 7.3 Monthly US Southwest border patrol encounters, October 2016 to September 2025

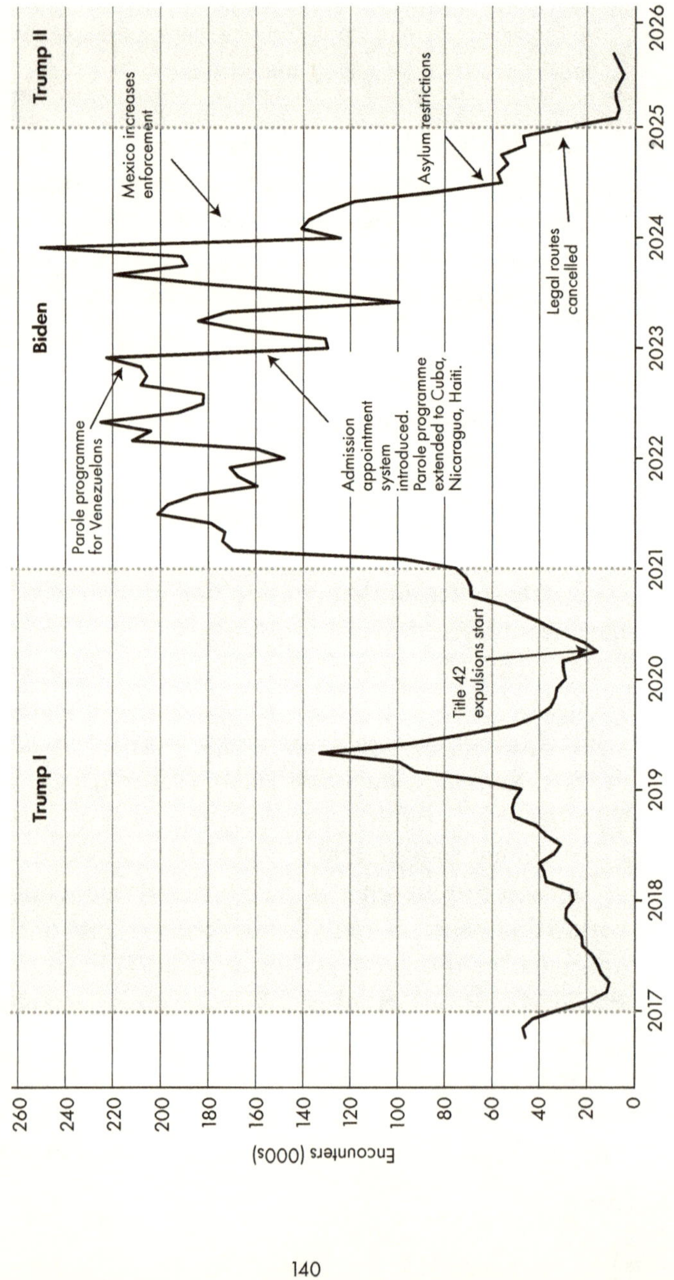

people who attempt to arrive without permission and apply for asylum in the normal way.

Let's focus on those who do qualify as refugees and who arrived without permission despite the government's attempts to deter them, as this is the most difficult challenge. A government that wants to ban territorial asylum really only has two options.

First, it can let the refugees remain in the country but refuse to grant them residence rights, hoping that without the right to work or settle long term, they will choose to leave. (This may contravene the Refugee Convention, which says refugees must receive various social and economic rights.) In practice, those who are actually refugees are unlikely to leave, as the alternative at home is even worse – although some may move on and try their luck in another country if they can.

Second, policymakers can find somewhere else to send refugees. In theory, they can ignore international law and send people back to their country of origin, where they may be harmed. Most policymakers do not want to do this, for either ethical or reputational reasons.[47] The alternative to the country of origin is a 'safe third country', in the jargon. Some people object to this on principle, because it involves forcing refugees to go somewhere they do not want to go – especially if it is not the third country they just crossed from but somewhere more distant where they have no connections. However, many scholars or moral philosophers who support refugee rights have proposed policies that would in practice involve moving refugees between safe countries against their will, as I discuss shortly.

The big challenge is finding countries that willing to accept more asylum seekers or refugees. The US under the Biden administration was able to rely on Mexico to prevent potential asylum seekers from reaching the US border and accept back deported nationals of Cuba, Haiti, Nicaragua and Venezuela in 2023 and 2024. However, when the Australian government announced it would not accept refugees who arrived without permission by boat, it struggled to find resettlement places them and a decade later many remained in limbo (see Box 7.4).

Can countries all agree to do things differently?

The Refugee Convention defined obligations towards refugees but provided no plan for sharing responsibility among states. The result has been a system predicated on disorderly migration and competition between nations to reduce exposure to refugees. Is there a better way?

Many people have proposed reforming the global protection system to make it clearer who is responsible for how many refugees.

What is a 'fair share' of refugees for each country to take? In theory, we could try to work this out by dividing the current number of refugees across potential destinations. For example, one study distributed responsibilities based on countries' population and wealth, and argued that to take their 'fair share', Australia would need to welcome another

400,000 refugees, the UK over 800,000 and the US six million, in addition to those they already hosted.[48]

The chances of high-income countries signing up to quotas of this size are basically zero. As a result, most proposals do not simply divide refugee numbers across countries per capita. Instead, they recognize that:

- Not all refugees need to be resettled to distant locations like the UK or Australia. People's skills may be better matched to the local economy in neighbouring countries with a similar level of economic development, and it will be easier for them to return home later if they can.[49]
- The cost of supporting refugees is much higher in high-income countries. In theory, wealthy countries can pay poorer countries to support refugees there.
- In any case, it is politically inconceivable that high-income countries will accept an even distribution of refugees across countries. With a few exceptions, they have spent decades trying to take as small a share of the world's refugees as they can.

One of the most famous proposals for shaking up the global refugee protection system comes from American law professor Peter Schuck. He argued for a system of 'tradable refugee quotas'. Under this system, an international agency would give a quota to each country based on factors such as their gross domestic product. But participating countries would not have to accept this number of refugees. Instead, they could pay other states to do so.

The option to pay other countries to fulfil their responsibility in theory enables a more 'efficient' distribution: countries more comfortable with refugees welcome larger numbers, while countries where public opinion is more hostile (such as Japan) do their bit by helping to prop the whole system up financially.

Some readers might be wrinkling their nose at the idea of a trade in refugees. Critics argue that this model commodifies human beings and denies refugees choice about where to settle. Is it dehumanizing? Yes, says Schuck. But so is the current system, where refugees choose between living in poverty or enforced idleness in neighbouring countries and making dangerous and unauthorized journeys to try their luck in another country's asylum system.

Would it work?

Imagine a global – or, more likely, regional – refugee agreement that substantially increased financial resources and resettlement places. Would this mean fewer refugees migrated through unauthorized routes? Very possibly, if the number of resettlement places in the new system was really big: big enough for applicants to feel they had a much better chance of securing legal status by going through legal routes.

If the new international system was not big enough to cater for all refugees, some would continue to move without authorization and claim refugee status. The ethical and political arguments for not sending refugees back to countries where they could be harmed would not disappear.

The quota system combines expanded legal routes with 'deterrence' in the form of forced relocations for people who moved outside the system. This sounds neat and tidy but it would have a brutal edge just like the current system. Refugees with sympathetic stories and family ties in the country would be forced onto planes heading for places they didn't want to live. This process would be difficult, expensive and harrowing for many of the individuals concerned. Though for many people it would be better than the status quo.

Is it politically realistic?

Why would states opt in to a system that gives them quotas of refugees? In theory, some countries that currently receive relatively few refugees might decide to welcome more if it meant fewer people coming on dangerous journeys into the asylum system. 'Safe and legal routes' may not help to reduce the number of asylum seekers if countries adopt them unilaterally, but a multilateral system might work if it were big enough. For countries that prioritize reducing the number of refugees coming through *any* route, the proposal looks less attractive. A large multilateral system would run up against the same constraint as a large unilateral one: destination countries' reluctance to accept larger numbers of refugees.

A new international system would require a huge leap of faith. Policymakers would need confidence that the system was really going to work. It would need smooth logistics and a big enough scale to deter people from moving without permission. It's impossible to say in advance how big that needs to be. If enough of the countries that have already managed to keep asylum applications low stayed out, others would be left to shoulder more of the burden. That could lead yet others to follow suit, letting the whole system unravel. All this might seem like a bit of a gamble, compared to muddling through with the status quo. That is one reason reform proposals have been floating around for decades without any serious negotiations on a large-scale agreement.

A less ambitious option is to stick with the Refugee Convention structure but reform it. For example, governments might be happy to clarify parts of the Convention that are not well defined, such as whether they can penalize people who arrive illegally if other safe routes or countries were available. This would not be easy either. Some people would want to narrow states' obligations while others would want to expand them. And the Refugee Convention is far from being the only show in town – others, such as the ECHR, also play a role. But it seems more feasible than entirely replacing the current global regime.

What is refugee policy for?

High-income countries have conflicting objectives in their policies towards refugees. On one hand, policymakers want to show that they are doing their bit for refugees. Publics don't want to feel that the country is mean-spirited or that innocent people will be put in harm's way.

On the other hand, policymakers also want to be able to select and control refugee arrivals – both to reduce the financial costs and to prioritize the refugees they consider more deserving or more politically popular. The Refugee Convention does not allow them to do this.

The result is a global asylum system in which governments grudgingly admit refugees who arrive though unauthorized, dangerous routes, while doing what they can to prevent them from arriving.

In theory, there may be ways for countries to cooperate to make refugee protection less reliant on unauthorized journeys. But producing such an agreement is no easy political feat. There is every risk the attempts would fail. It may simply not be possible to shoehorn all asylum migration into neatly organized 'safe and legal routes' even if in theory this might be desirable. Ultimately, the biggest problem with the Refugee Convention – its failure to define how responsibilities for refugees should be shared – may be the thing that has made it just about acceptable to so many countries for so long.

8
CONCLUSION

Imagine you are the Interior Minister in a wealthy democracy. You've just been voted into office promising a 'fair and controlled' immigration policy and now it's time to lay out some details. But first, a few meetings.

The Finance Minister wants a word: public finances are tight and the country can't afford any reduction in skilled migration. The Health Secretary drops by: on no account can you restrict migration in the care sector – the health system couldn't cope with the strain. The Trade Minister is preparing for negotiations with some important migration origin countries: perhaps a new scheme for their citizens could be introduced? The Education Minister says universities will collapse if you don't keep the door open to international students. The Culture Department wants more generous rules for artists and musicians, the Agriculture Ministry wants a bigger seasonal worker programme, the Foreign Affairs Ministry is reluctant to backtrack on previous commitments to refugees. Meanwhile, colleagues from across the country keep bringing you cases of constituents who are separated from their partners by the immigration rules.

Is there anything left? If you said yes to all these requests immigration would greatly increase, but you were voted into office saying that immigration was already quite high enough. All these choices will add up.

Perhaps you can hire some independent experts to advise on the right level of migration and work back from there? Afraid not: the experts say this is a political choice (see Box 8.1).

Box 8.1: Is there a 'right' amount of migration?

Migration has many different impacts: on society and culture, public finances, the housing market, public services, local communities, and citizens with non-citizen partners, friends and colleagues. Some people benefit more than others. Crucially, many of the impacts of migration depend on who migrates, not just how many. They also depend on how the destination country responds – for example, how many new homes it builds or how well it helps migrants to settle in.

All this makes it difficult to add the impacts up and determine an optimal level of migration in any scientific way. That doesn't mean numbers are irrelevant. Numbers affect the pace of social change. They also affect the housing market, if there

> are constraints on building new homes. But the complexity of the impacts means that decisions about migration levels are a political judgement rather than an evidence-based science. Views on the appropriate level of migration will depend a lot on who you are asking.

Three different visions of what immigration policy is for

At this stage in any book about public policy it is customary to set out a path to a happier place that sensibly resolves the trade-offs and that is impeccably rooted in the evidence. The problem is, as I hope this book has shown, it's not that easy. None of the policies fully achieve their goals, and all have winners and losers. Your vision for migration will depend on what you prioritize.

Here are some hypothetical examples of what policymakers might do if they prioritized different outcomes. It is by no means an exhaustive list of potential migration strategies, but aims to capture some of the most common debates.

Option 1: Prioritizing low migration

Some governments and citizens prioritize reducing migration levels, often to slow social change or population growth, or address concerns about pressure on housing or infrastructure. What does the low-migration vision look like in practice?

CONCLUSION

First, it probably involves a minimal number of work visas. Work migration is often operationally easiest to cut, if something has to go. A reasonably large share of work visas might be strictly temporary, so that they do not contribute much to long-term growth in the migrant population.

Second, family migration policy would also need to be restrictive, since in many countries this is the largest long-term migration category. Parents, siblings and other relatives would not be permitted at all, or only under narrow circumstances. Partners of citizens would face income and language requirements. Policymakers would have to decide how tough these would be. The higher these requirements, the more often citizens would face separation from their non-citizen partners – the consequences of which can be devastating for the families themselves.

Third, low-migration policymakers would not voluntarily resettle many refugees. They would do what they could to restrict people from arriving to claim asylum, using policies such as visa restrictions and physical enforcement. If geography made physical enforcement difficult, they would try to negotiate with other countries to accept asylum seekers who had arrived spontaneously – most obviously, any neighbouring countries people passed through before making asylum claims. Where they could, they would negotiate with countries of origin to return refused asylum seekers. In practice, geography and geopolitics would have a big impact on their ability to reduce asylum migration.

Would policymakers contribute financially to the global refugee protection system? It depends whether they thought high-income countries and their citizens had a responsibility towards refugees displaced in countries beyond their immediate borders. If they did not, they would leave the task of supporting refugees to other countries, and hope those countries were willing and able to do it. If they did feel they had a role globally, they might instead decide to contribute financially to supporting refugees elsewhere.

A low-migration strategy does not have to mean that migrants who do receive residence permits are treated poorly. Policymakers can combine restrictive rules for entry visas with policies designed to support migrants to settle in. This could include low application fees, subsidies for language learning, or support to become a citizen.

The low-migration scenario brings a slower pace of social and cultural change, lower population growth, and more time for infrastructure and housing to adjust to that growth. It comes with trade-offs. There are human costs, particularly for citizens with non-citizen partners and for refugees whom deterrence policies failed to deter. Restricting highly skilled migration would have economic costs. Those costs might be offset to some extent by the potential fiscal benefit of restrictions on asylum, but only if those restrictions actually worked.

Box 8.2: Numerical limits on migration

A commonly proposed strategy for reducing migration is to introduce numerical limits. For example, the US caps the number of green cards in many subcategories, such as work visas and siblings of US citizens.

If a cap is oversubscribed, one of two things happens: a backlog builds up, or some people who qualify for the visa are rejected. These consequences are the reason many policymakers do not like capping migration. The people who have visas rejected due to the cap will not necessarily be the ones policymakers or the public least wanted to admit. Backlogs impose waiting times on prospective migrants, their employers or their families. For example, some people in the US wait decades for a green card to become available. If policymakers want lower migration, it will typically be more efficient simply to accept that some groups of people will no longer qualify for visas.

The main argument in favour of caps is that politicians often say they want to reduce migration but aren't really serious about doing it. They will only stop issuing visas when a hard limit forces them to. Caps thus reflect mistrust of immigration policymakers' ability to demonstrate control.

Option 2: Prioritizing economics

What if policymakers' main goal was instead to maximize the economic benefits of migration? First and most obviously, economics-oriented policymakers would take a liberal approach to migrant workers in high-skilled jobs. They might even admit some workers without job offers already lined up, to make it easier for them to find skilled work (for example on a job-search visa). They would also collect all the data they needed to check that their policies were genuinely admitting people who held down skilled jobs in the long term.

Second, policymakers prioritizing economics might introduce strictly temporary visas for jobs at the low to middle end of the skills spectrum, with no option for those workers to bring family members.

Third, a purely economic migration strategy would be restrictive towards refugees. It would do almost no voluntary resettlement or 'safe and legal routes' – such as resettlement from conflict zones or the visas for Ukrainians that some countries introduced after the Russian invasion in 2022. At most, it might offer some visa pathways for refugees with skilled job offers.

Policymakers would implement the more cost-effective strategies that physically prevent asylum seekers from reaching their territory, such as visa restrictions. The economics of asylum deterrence policies is less straightforward: working out which ones break even financially requires wildly speculative assumptions, so policymakers in this scenario might disagree on how to proceed.

Similarly, 'economics-first' policymakers would impose socio-economic requirements on the partners of citizens, although they might struggle to identify the level that optimizes economic outcomes in a rational way. They would not allow their citizens' elderly parents to migrate.

Finally, a migration strategy designed to maximize economic benefits might find ways to tax migrants more – either through visa fees or income taxes. It would probably restrict access to benefits, though not necessarily for long-term migrants with children (since growing up in poverty imposes long-term costs). Policies to support migrants' economic and social wellbeing will be those most likely to have an economic return, such as helping skilled family migrants get their qualifications recognized.

The economics-first strategy also comes with trade-offs. In this scenario, policymakers would be willing to impose some of the same human costs as we saw in the low-migration scenario, except that they might want more solid evidence that policies to deter asylum seekers or restrict citizens' family members would pay off economically. People on temporary visas with few rights would face the risk of exploitation, and migrants facing higher fees and taxes without a welfare safety net might be less able to participate fully in society – potentially generating unintended economic costs in the longer term.

Option 3: Prioritizing humanitarian concerns

A third approach prioritizes the rights and wellbeing of migrants themselves, even if that means higher migration levels or larger economic costs.

Different visions for a more humane immigration system exist. At one extreme is a system in which governments no longer prioritize the preferences of citizens over prospective migrants. This logic takes us to an open-borders policy. This would be politically unpopular, and thus unlikely to survive for long in any of today's high-income democratic nation states. The main task facing policymakers who wanted to pursue this option would be to persuade citizens it was a good idea (see Box 8.4).

An alternative humanitarian approach still prioritizes the preferences of people living in the country (whether citizens or non-citizens) over prospective migrants, restricting new migration to some extent.

Policymakers in this scenario would be liberal on family migration, which benefits the citizen family members who are already resident.

Policymakers would not necessarily have a strong view on the level of work migration. But people who *did* receive work visas – alongside others such as family migrants – would get more rights. This might include rapid access to permanent status and to the welfare safety net. Application fees would be low and decisions fast. The paperwork would be simple and case workers would give applicants the benefit of the doubt – implicitly tolerating a certain amount of immigration fraud as the quid pro quo.

CONCLUSION

Policies that prioritize being humane would treat asylum seekers well once they arrived in the country. They would grant asylum to a relatively high share of applicants, erring on the side of accepting claims that may be ineligible in order to avoid rejecting true claims. Policymakers would not impose deterrence policies that involve restricting rights or increasing risks of poverty for asylum seekers or refugees. Would this system still try to physically prevent people from arriving? This might be a matter of some debate. If it did not, asylum migration would greatly increase – particularly if other countries continued their efforts to deter and prevent asylum applications.

Policymakers might decide to operate 'safe routes' for refugees to arrive without making dangerous and unauthorized journeys. They shouldn't expect these to have much impact on the number of people attempting to seek asylum through the usual routes – that is, using unauthorized journeys. Policymakers might see safe routes instead as a way of helping to prop up the international refugee protection system and reducing the pressure on countries bordering conflict zones.

Humanitarian-focused policymakers would take a relatively liberal approach to legalizing unauthorized migrants. They would realistically need at least some enforcement. However, they might seek to focus on penalizing *employers* who recruit people without the right to work, more than migrants themselves.

Finally, government would support migrants after they arrive with other policies that help them settle in, such as subsidized language lessons.

What trade-offs come with the humanitarian strategy? Readers may have noticed that many of its components are the opposite of the 'prioritizing economics' choices. This is one reason why migration scholar Martin Ruhs talks about the 'price of rights': rights may be socially desirable, but they are often not economically beneficial.* Because the humanitarian strategy probably involves relatively high levels of migration, it also implies a faster pace of social change; some citizens would be fine with this, and others would not.

> **Box 8.3: Can policymakers compensate people who oppose high migration?**
>
> Some scholars argue that instead of reducing migration, policymakers should accept that migration has winners and losers and focus on mitigating any negative consequences for those who lose out.
>
> When the costs and benefits are economic, in theory it should be feasible to compensate people who lose out financially. In practice, that is complicated because the negative economic impacts of higher migration are generally quite diffuse. For example, high migration may contribute to rising

---

* Restrictions on rights are not always good for the economy. For example, detaining unauthorized migrants or asylum seekers is expensive. Letting children live in poverty can be costly in the long run too.

> housing costs across the country, and not only in the highest-migration areas. Governments operating a high-migration strategy might decide to remove barriers to homebuilding, in countries where new construction is difficult. This might involve overruling objections to development, including those that are justifiable on other grounds (for example, the desire to preserve green spaces).
>
> However, many people's concerns about migration are not economic, but social and cultural. In theory, some policies might help reduce the social impacts of migration, such as supporting language learning. That said, policymakers' ability to influence the way people experience social change naturally has its limits.

None of these three visions aligns perfectly with what a single country does. Japan traditionally came close to the 'low migration' vision, although it has liberalized its policies in recent years. Australia arguably best fits the 'economics first' vision, although it has not pursued all of the options for restricting family migration. And for a long time, Sweden matched much of the humanitarian policy vision, despite some recent restrictions.

The same country does not always stick to the same path. For example, the UK swung between periods of more liberal and more restrictive policies from the mid-2000s to the mid-2020s. Increasing migration is easier than reducing it, however, both operationally and politically. A well-established phenomenon in political science is that once a programme already exists, it develops supporters who fight any move to close it.[1] Restrictions on migration often have smaller effects than expected, because people adapt to the new rules and find ways to become eligible. Countries that already have substantial migrant populations have economic and social links with origin countries, which encourages further migration in future. These are among the reasons almost every high-income democracy in the world has seen increases in the foreign-born share of the population since 1990.[2] Exceptionally few have seen decreases, even among countries that are often cited as restrictive, such as Denmark or Hungary.

Can politicians do better?

In democracies, politicians have to sell their policies to the public. Between elections, politicians and advocates compete to secure legitimacy by claiming that their preferred set of policies is 'what the public wants'. People who prioritize migrants' rights tell us the public want compassion. People who prioritize a slower pace of social change say the public support control and lower numbers. Those who prioritize economic benefits tell us the public wants skill-selective policies.

They are all right: the public want many different things. They can't have them all – at least, not to the same degree and not all at once. People say they want lower migration, but when asked about specific groups – nurses, students, family members – they often support more liberal policies. In other words, many citizens want something impossible: liberal immigration policies that deliver low migration.[3] That might just about be possible in some destinations, but not in sought-after high-income countries like the UK, US or Australia.

The tension between support for lower migration and support for individual migration categories makes life very difficult for politicians who want to please the public. Public support for a particular policy will depend on how it is framed, and that can change over time. Framing that focuses on the lives of the people affected by migration policy tends to encourage more liberal views, while framing that focuses on the aggregate numbers and consequences will encourage more restrictive ones. Politicians can influence the framing, but they do not control it: they are at the mercy of events.

One of the most dramatic about-turns in recent history was the public outcry in Europe after seeing photographs of the body of two-year-old Alan Kurdi, a Syrian boy who drowned as his family tried to cross the Mediterranean. Any migration expert knew that the journey to Europe was dangerous and many people were dying, including children. But it took an emotive photo for Europe to shift to a brief period of 'ecstatic humanitarianism', in the words of one study of media coverage in 2015 in eight European Union (EU) countries.[4] Media stories after Alan's death became more likely to highlight individual refugee voices. Sentiment shifted abruptly again just after two months later after the Bataclan terrorist attack in Paris. Media then focused much less on emotions and shifted back to a more distant framing, focusing on geopolitical risks.*

How should politicians deal with the tension between public demand for low migration and liberal migration policies at the same time? In an ideal world, perhaps they would honestly and explicitly lay out the trade-offs, explaining how their chosen policies have balanced competing objectives. But do voters actually reward them for doing this? In the short run, probably not. In the short run, they have an incentive to promise low migration without actually delivering it.

A vivid illustration of this problem comes from successive Conservative governments in the UK from 2010 to 2024. Government ministers repeatedly promised dramatic reductions in net migration – that is, immigration minus emigration – from the hundreds of thousands to the 'tens of thousands'. While they did introduce restrictions in 2010–2012, the plans were clearly nowhere near sufficient to reduce migration as much as they had promised.[5] Under Prime Minister Boris Johnson, a government re-elected with a pledge to reduce net migration accidentally allowed it to triple, following a series of liberalizing policy choices – including new routes for care workers and international students that attracted many more migrants than anticipated.

---

* The Bataclan attackers were largely Muslim EU citizens rather than recent asylum seekers, although some were reported to have travelled back to the EU from the Middle East alongside asylum seekers via unauthorized routes.

CONCLUSION

In the long run, making promises with no clear plan to meet them is a recipe for disillusionment. Politicians may be able to tie their own hands – and the hands of their successors – by establishing processes that force them to make the trade-offs explicit. For example, the governments in Canada and Australia publicly announce planned levels of migration within each category and overall. Policymakers can invite public scrutiny by commissioning independent evaluations, producing better data, or publishing policy impact assessments when policies are introduced. These things will not force all policymakers to be honest about trade-offs, but they may chip away at the problem at the margins.

> **Box 8.4: Can advocates persuade the public to change their minds?**
>
> Politicians and advocates on all sides of the debate naturally want to bring more people over to their point of view. In democracies, public support is crucial to legitimacy in the long term.
>
> Quite a few studies have looked at whether people change their minds when they receive positive or negative information about migration policies. For example, US survey evidence suggests respondents often think immigration policies are more liberal than they really are – for example, that people could qualify to immigrate as an aunt or uncle of a

US citizen – and that they are more likely to support liberal policies if they are told that current policies are restrictive.[6] Similarly, political rhetoric and media portrayals that criticize migration or disparage migrants can activate support for restrictive policies.[7]

Migration scholar Alexander Kustov argues that what really persuades voters is not rhetoric, but the government introducing policies that are *demonstrably beneficial* – particularly policies that prioritize skilled migration.[8] He argues that liberal democracies may be able to sneak some refugee resettlement into the mix too, if the overall policy package is clearly skill-selective – although there are few countries other than Canada that have done this, making it hard to judge the likely impacts in other settings.

Studies on the impacts of persuasion often take place in experimental settings rather than the real world. In the real world, voters are not always paying much attention. It's fair enough – they are busy living their lives. The lack of public knowledge about what immigration policies actually do is one reason that successive governments in the UK announced the introduction of an 'Australian-style points-based system' no fewer than three times between 2002 and 2019 – without many people experiencing déjà vu. And indeed without even introducing a system that bore much resemblance to the Australian one.

CONCLUSION

The differences between competing visions of what immigration policy should be for are fundamental and values-based. Doing a better job at laying out the trade-offs will not dissolve the disagreements away, although some compromises are possible. For example, one recent German study found that the largest number of poll respondents supported a position that restricted entry more than liberals would like, but offered migrants more rights after arrival than sceptics would like – such as faster access to permanent status and welfare benefits.[9]

Even if there is no single right answer, there are some things that perhaps we can all agree on. First, we shouldn't dismiss the benefits of good old-fashioned competence. Inattention to the dull business of competently running the asylum system was a major factor behind the spiralling asylum backlog in the UK between 2018 and 2022, for example. The EU's 'Dublin' system for determining which EU Member State was responsible for which asylum seekers may have sounded sensible on paper but got bogged down in poor implementation and politics. Failure to think through how 'investor visa' policies should work meant that programmes in Australia, Canada and the UK ended up admitting rich housewives and retirees instead of the entrepreneurial businesspeople policymakers had envisaged.

Policymakers may like to present their policies as radical solutions, and innovative experiments have their place. But improvements can also come from tweaks at the margins that will not get anyone's heartbeat racing. For example, after the mid-2010s, Canada, Australia and New Zealand all started using 'expression of interest' systems to manage the way they used points tests to select skilled work migrants. This is a way of gathering and ranking immigration applications, before inviting people to apply only if they are likely to be successful. This saves migrants, employers and the government work, and reduced the problem of inefficient and costly backlogs. However, I didn't even discuss this development in the chapter on skilled work migration, because it might have made too many readers fall asleep.

Least sexy of all, but incredibly important: collecting data. Norwegian policymakers can pick through detailed data on everything from the taxes paid by migrants on different visa types, to the educational performance of migrants' children and the rates of incarceration by immigration status. But in many European countries, the data that policymakers would need to know whether their policies work simply isn't collected. For example, until 2025 the UK no idea what hundreds of thousands of people admitted as partners of work and study visa holders were doing in the labour market – or almost anything else about them, for that matter.

Many immigration policies have barely been evaluated. For example, policies designed to require employers to look for local recruits before hiring someone from overseas on a work visa are common, but as of 2025 there was almost no evidence on whether they work. All high-income countries use immigration detention at least to some extent, but some would like to rely on it less because of the financial and human cost. However, it is surprisingly hard to find rigorous evidence on how likely migrants are to abscond before being removed if they are not detained.

Lack of evidence appears to be no barrier to widespread adoption of new policies. In fact, policies sometimes spread like wildfire despite evidence that they tend *not* to work – like investor visas in Europe after the financial crisis. Advocates on all sides proclaim that 'other countries are doing this' as if that alone showed it was a good idea.

Finally, while we cannot expect everyone to agree about migration policy, we can all contribute to a more honest, measured debate. As humans, we often feel confident that we are right and that people who disagree with us are wrong.[10] This makes it tempting to vilify opponents as ignorant or evil. But to justify their preferred policies, it is not necessary for sceptics to show that asylum seekers or 'leftie lawyers' are bad people abusing the system. Liberals proposing greater rights for migrants do not need to argue that migration restrictions are inherently racist, either. If we spend too much time playing the man rather than the ball, the debate simply becomes more polarized and there is less time for actually diagnosing the problems and agreeing how to address them.

In a more measured debate, people with liberal views on migration might accept that not all migration is economically beneficial; that rules are inevitably going to need to be enforced even though the consequences for individuals can be harsh; and that people do not have to be prejudiced to want a slower pace of social change. People with sceptical views might recognize that many migrants contribute both economically and socially; that people who apply for and receive asylum are not 'gaming the system' but simply using the rules in the way they were designed to work; and that the human suffering caused by restrictions on family migration is real.

Both sides might recognize that the large majority of migrants are neither saints nor sinners – they are ordinary people living their lives. And everyone would accept that there are trade-offs, that some problems have no easy solution, and that people with opposing viewpoints are not wicked: they just have a different vision of what is right – and therefore what immigration policy is for.

NOTES

Chapter 1

1. B. Anderson, *Us and Them? The Dangerous Politics of Immigration Control* (Oxford University Press, 2013).
2. Kantar Public and Migration Observatory, *Public Attitudes to Immigration 2023* (Kantar Public, 2023). https://kantar.turtl.co/story/public-attitudes-to-immigration/page/1.
3. J.R. Dinwiddy, 'The Use of the Crown's Power of Deportation Under the Aliens Act, 1793–1826', *Historical Research* 41, no. 104 (1968), pp. 193–211. https://academic.oup.com/histres/article-abstract/41/104/193/5678326?redirectedFrom=fulltext.
4. C.J. Gibbs, 'Friends and Enemies: The Underground War between Great Britain and France, 1793–1802', ch. 2, *The Napoleon Series*, January 2011. https://www.napoleon-series.org/research/government/british/Espionage/c_espionageintro.html.
5. B. Conrad and M. Křížová, *Borders in Early Modern History* (OpenBook Publishers, 2023). https://books.openbookpublishers.com/10.11647/obp.0323/ch4.xhtml.
6. T. Lewis, 'Transatlantic Slave Trade', *Encyclopædia Britannica*. https://www.britannica.com/topic/transatlantic-slave-trade.
7. Aliens Act 1905, enacted 11 August 1905. https://www.legislation.gov.uk/ukpga/Edw7/5/13/contents/enacted.
8. C.H. Wellman and P. Cole, 'Introduction', in C.H. Wellman and P. Cole (eds), *Debating the Ethics of Immigration: Is There a Right to Exclude?* (New York, 2011), pp. 1–10. https://doi.org/10.1093/acprof:osobl/9780199731732.003.0001.
9. T. Pogge, *Poverty and Human Rights*. https://www.palermo.edu/Archivos_content/2015/derecho/pobreza_multidimensional/bibliografia/Sesion3_doc3.pdf
10. C. Besteman, Militarized Global Apartheid, *Current Anthropology*, 60.S19 (2019): S26–S38J. https://www.journals.uchicago.edu/doi/full/10.1086/699280.

11. B. Caplan and Z. Weinersmith, *Open Borders: The Science and Ethics of Immigration* (St Martin's Press, 2019).
12. D. Miller, 'Is There a Human Right to Immigrate? (Final Draft)', CSSJ Working Papers Series, SJ033, April 2015. https://www.politics.ox.ac.uk/sites/default/files/inline-files/SJ033.pdf.
13. World Values Survey, 'UK Attitudes to Immigration among Most Positive Internationally', 2023. https://www.uk-values.org/news-comment/uk-attitudes-to-immigration-among-most-positive-internationally-1018742/pub01-115.
14. K. Natter, 'Autocratic Immigration Policymaking: The Illiberal Paradox Hypothesis', International Migration Institute, 2024. https://www.migrationinstitute.org/publications/autocratic-immigration-policymaking-the-illiberal-paradox-hypothesis. See also: D.S. FitzGerald and D. Cook-Martín, *Culling the Masses: The Democratic Origins of Racist Immigration Policy in the Americas* (Harvard University Press, 2014).
15. Migration Observatory, 'Migrants in the UK: An Overview', 9 August 2024. https://migrationobservatory.ox.ac.uk/resources/briefings/migrants-in-the-uk-an-overview/.
16. M. Blauberger, A. Heindlmaier, P. Hofmarcher, J. Assmus and B. Mitter, 'The Differentiated Politicization of Free Movement of People in the EU: A Topic Model Analysis of Press Coverage in Austria, Germany, Poland and the UK', *Journal of European Public Policy*, 30, no. 2 (2023), pp. 291–314. https://www.tandfonline.com/doi/full/10.1080/13501763.2021.1986118#d1e851.
17. J. Dennison and N. Carl, 'The Ultimate Causes of Brexit: History, Culture, and Geography', *LSE Research Online*, 2017. https://eprints.lse.ac.uk/71492/1/blogs.lse.ac.uk-The%20ultimate%20causes%20of%20Brexit%20history%20culture%20and%20geography.pdf.
18. International Organization for Migration, *World Migration Report 2024*, Interactive Edition. https://worldmigrationreport.iom.int/msite/wmr-2024-interactive/.
19. UN DESA, 'International Migrants Numbered 272 Million in 2019, Continuing an Upward Trend in All Major World Regions', *Population Facts*, no. 2019/4, September 2019. https://www.un.org/en/development/desa/population/migration/publications/populationfacts/docs/MigrationStock2019_PopFacts_2019-04.pdf.
20. G. Younge, 'Ambalavaner Sivanandan Obituary', *The Guardian*, 7 February 2018. https://www.theguardian.com/world/2018/feb/07/ambalavaner-sivanandan.

NOTES

21 W. MacAskill, K. Bykvist and T. Ord, *Moral Uncertainty* (Oxford University Press, 2020), p. 240.

Chapter 2

1 A. Edo and C. Özgüzel, 'The Impact of Immigration on the Employment Dynamics of European Regions', *Labour Economics* 85 (2023), Article 102613. https://www.sciencedirect.com/science/article/pii/S0927537123001082.

2 C. Nedoncelle, L. Marchal, A. Aubry and J. Héricourt, 'Does Immigration Affect Native Wages? A Meta-analysis', KCG Working Paper No. 31, 2024. https://www.econstor.eu/handle/10419/281775.

3 C. Dustmann, Y. Kastis and I. Preston, 'Inequality and Immigration', Institute for Fiscal Studies, November 2022. https://www.nuffieldfoundation.org/wp-content/uploads/2019/11/Inequality-and-immigration-IFS-Deaton-Review-of-Inequalities.pdf#page=23.

4 E.W.F. Peterson, 'The Role of Population in Economic Growth', *SAGE Open* 7, no. 4 (2017). https://journals.sagepub.com/doi/full/10.1177/2158244017736094.

5 On the difference between low and high-skilled migration, see R. Fabling, D.C. Maré and P. Stevens, 'Migration and Firm-level Productivity', IZA Discussion Paper No. 15482, 2023. https://docs.iza.org/dp15482.pdf. On low-skilled migration reducing technology adoption, see L. Liu and A. Portes, 'Immigration and Robots: Is the Absence of Immigrants Linked to the Rise of Automation?', *Ethnic and Racial Studies* 44, no. 15 (2021), pp. 2723–2751. https://www.tandfonline.com/doi/full/10.1080/01419870.2020.1849757 and E. Lewis, 'Immigration, Skill Mix, and Capital Skill Complementarity', *The Quarterly Journal of Economics* 126, no. 2 (2011), pp. 1029–1069. https://academic.oup.com/qje/article-abstract/126/2/1029/1869919. On task specialization, see, for example, G. Peri and C. Sparber, 'Task Specialization, Immigration, and Wages', *American Economic Journal: Applied Economics* 1, no. 3 (2009), pp. 135–169. https://www.jstor.org/stable/25760175.

6 Migration Advisory Committee, *EEA Migration in the UK: Final Report*, 2018, pp. 55–59. https://assets.publishing.service.gov.uk/media/5ba26c1de5274a54d5c39be2/Final_EEA_report.PDF.

7 T. Hall and A. Manning, *Only Human? Immigration and Firm Productivity in Britain*, Centre for Economic Performance Discussion Paper No. 2060, 2024. https://cep.lse.ac.uk/pubs/download/dp2060.pdf; Office for Budget Responsibility, *Economic*

    and Fiscal Outlook: March 2024, 6 March 2024. https://obr.uk/efo/economic-and-fiscal-outlook-march-2024/.
8   Office for Budget Responsibility, *Fiscal Risks and Sustainability Report*, September 2024. https://obr.uk/frs/fiscal-risks-and-sustainability-september-2024/#chapter-4.
9   S. Webb, 'Was Multi-culturalism a Conservative Idea?', *Substack*, 31 January 2025. https://sfhwebb.substack.com/p/was-multi-culturalism-a-conservative.
10 A.F. Rasmussen, 'Prime Minister Anders Fogh Rasmussen's Address at the Opening of the Session of the Folketing on 7 October 2003', 2003. https://english.stm.dk/the-prime-minister/speeches/prime-minister-anders-fogh-rasmussen-s-address-at-the-opening-of-the-session-of-the-folketing-on-7-october-2003/.
11 J. Hainmueller and D.J. Hopkins, 'Public Attitudes toward Immigration', *Annual Review of Political Science* 17 (2014), pp. 225–249.
12 A. Kustov, *In Our Interest: How Democracies Can Make Immigration Popular* (Columbia University Press, 2025).
13 A. Heath and L. Richards, *Attitudes Towards Immigration and their Antecedents*, European Social Survey Topline Results Series, Issue 7, June 2023. https://www.europeansocialsurvey.org/sites/default/files/2023-06/TL7-Immigration-English.pdf, p. 8.
14 P.T. Dinesen, M. Schaeffer and K.M. Sønderskov, 'Ethnic Diversity and Social Trust: A Narrative and Meta-Analytical Review', *Annual Review of Political Science* 23 (2020) 441–465. https://www.annualreviews.org/content/journals/10.1146/annurev-polisci-052918-020708; M. Abascal and D. Baldassarri, 'Love Thy Neighbor? Ethnoracial Diversity and Trust Reexamined', *American Journal of Sociology* 121, no. 3 (2015), pp. 722–782. https://pubmed.ncbi.nlm.nih.gov/26900618/.
15 E.F.P. Luttmer, 'Group Loyalty and the Taste for Redistribution', *Journal of Political Economy* 109, no. 3 (2001), pp. 500–528. https://www.journals.uchicago.edu/doi/abs/10.1086/321019; C.D. Batson, J.G. Batson, R.M. Todd, B.H. Brummett, L.L. Shaw and C.M.R. Aldeguer, 'Empathy and the Collective Good: Caring for One of the Others in a Social Dilemma', *Journal of Personality and Social Psychology* 68, no. 4 (1995), pp. 619–631. https://psycnet.apa.org/record/1995-25033-001.
16 M. Nathan, 'After Florida: Towards an Economics of Diversity', *European Urban and Regional Studies* 22, no. 1 (2015), pp. 3–19. https://journals.sagepub.com/doi/abs/10.1177/0969776412463371.

NOTES

17 M. Fernández-Reino, 'The Health of Migrants in the UK', 31 August 2020. https://migrationobservatory.ox.ac.uk/resources/briefings/the-health-of-migrants-in-the-uk/.

18 M. Beek and F. Fleischmann, 'Religion and Integration: Does Immigrant Generation Matter? The Case of Moroccan and Turkish Immigrants in the Netherlands', *Journal of Ethnic and Migration Studies* 46, no. 17 (2020), pp. 3655–3676. https://doi.org/10.1080/1369183X.2019.1620417; M. Fernández-Reino and B. Brindle, 'Migrants in the UK Labour Market: An Overview', 16 June 2025, Figure 10. https://migrationobservatory.ox.ac.uk/resources/briefings/migrants-in-the-uk-labour-market-an-overview/.

19 Pew Research Center, 'Global Divide on Homosexuality Persists', June 2020. https://www.pewresearch.org/global/2020/06/25/global-divide-on-homosexuality-persists/; A. Roder and N. Spierings, 'What Shapes Attitudes Toward Homosexuality among European Muslims? The Role of Religiosity and Destination Hostility', *International Migration Review* 56, no. 2 (2021), pp. 533–561. https://journals.sagepub.com/doi/10.1177/01979183211041288

20 L. Pessin and B. Arpino, 'Navigating Between Two Cultures: Immigrants' Gender Attitudes Toward Working Women', *Demographic Research* 38 (2018), pp. 967–1016. https://www.demographic-research.org/volumes/vol38/35/38-35.pdf.

21 C. Dawson, M. Veliziotis and B. Hopkins, 'Assimilation of the Migrant Work Ethic', Economics Working Paper Series 1407, University of the West of England, 2014. https://www2.uwe.ac.uk/faculties/BBS/BUS/Research/Economics%20Papers%202014/1407.pdf

22 S.M. Plenty and J.O. Jonsson, 'Students' Occupational Aspirations: Can Family Relationships Account for Differences Between Immigrant and Socioeconomic Groups?', *Child Development* 92, no. 1 (2021), pp. 157–173. https://ora.ox.ac.uk/objects/uuid:6c497fde-114b-41d5-bfad-70f2168b9340/files/rdf65v812m.

23 S. Burgess, 'Understanding the Success of London's Schools', Working Paper No. 14/333, The Centre for Market and Public Organisation, 2014. https://www.bristol.ac.uk/media-library/sites/cmpo/migrated/documents/wp333.pdf.

24 S.J. Turnbull-Dugarte and A. López Ortega, 'Instrumentally Inclusive: The Political Psychology of Homonationalism', *American Political Science Review* 118, no. 3 (2024), pp. 1360–1378. https://www.cambridge.org/core/journals/american-political-science-review/article/instrumentally-inclusive-the-political-

psychology-of-homonationalism/1D9425F6FA20F34B0918018
275A507A8; S. van Oosten, 'Which Voters Stereotype Muslim
Politicians as Homophobic?', *The Loop*, 27 June 2023.
https://theloop.ecpr.eu/which-voters-stereotype-muslim-politicians-
as-homophobic/; J. Johansson and J. Dashti, 'Femonationalism in
the Civic-integration Work Conducted by a Swedish NGO with
Men's Groups', *NORMA* 19, no. 4 (2024), pp. 230–245.
https://www.tandfonline.com/doi/full/10.1080/18902138
.2024.2411795.

25 A. Röder, 'Immigrants' Attitudes toward Homosexuality:
Socialization, Religion, and Acculturation in European Host
Societies', *International Migration Review* 49, no. 4 (2015),
pp. 1042–1070.

26 M.R. Ramos, M.R. Bennett, D.S. Massey and M. Hewstone,
'Humans Adapt to Social Diversity over Time', *PNAS* 116, no. 25
(2019), pp. 12244–12249. https://www.pnas.org/doi/abs/10.1073/
pnas.1818884116.

27 P. Connor and M. Koenig, 'Explaining the Muslim Employment
Gap in Western Europe: Individual-level Effects and Ethno-
religious Penalties', *Social Science Research* 49 (2015),
pp. 191–201. https://www.sciencedirect.com/science/article/pii/
S0049089X14001562?via%3Dihub.

28 L. Lucassen, 'Immigration, Intermarriage and the Changing Face
of Europe in the Post War Period', *History of the Family* 14, no. 1
(2009), pp. 52–68. https://scholarlypublications.universiteitleiden
.nl/handle/1887/15000

29 Ibid.

30 A. Röder, 'Immigrants' Attitudes toward Homosexuality:
Socialization, Religion, and Acculturation in European Host
Societies', *International Migration Review* 49, no. 4 (2015),
pp. 1042–1070.

31 United States Census Bureau, 'American Community Survey table
S0201 Selected Population Profile in the United States'. https://data
.census.gov/table/ACSSPP1Y2023.S0201?t=-B0:Income+and+
Poverty&moe=false.

32 N. Foner and R. Alba, 'Immigrant Religion in the U.S. and Western
Europe: Bridge or Barrier to Inclusion?', *International Migration
Review* 42, no. 1 (2008), pp. 360–392. https://onlinelibrary.wiley
.com/doi/full/10.1111/j.1747-7379.2008.00128.x#b29.

33 Office for National Statistics, 'England and Wales Census 2021'.
https://www.ons.gov.uk/datasets/create; Migration Policy Institute;

NOTES

J. Batalova, 'Mexican Immigrants in the United States', *Migration Information Source*, 8 October 2024. https://www.migrationpolicy.org/article/mexican-immigrants-united-states.

34 C. Adida, D. Laitin and M.-A. Valfort, 'The Struggle to Integrate Muslims in Europe', 2023. https://immigrationlab.org/project/the-struggle-to-integrate-muslims-in-europe/.

35 M. Rizzo, S. Testa, S. Gattino and A. Miglietta, 'Religiously Flexible: Acculturation of Second-generation Muslims in Europe', *International Journal of Intercultural Relations* 91 (2022), pp. 127–137. https://www.sciencedirect.com/science/article/pii/S0147176722001171.

36 S. Ghumman and A.M. Ryan, 'Not Welcome Here: Discrimination towards Women who Wear the Muslim Headscarf', *Human Relations* 66, no. 5 (2013), pp. 671–698. https://journals.sagepub.com/doi/full/10.1177/0018726712469540; Pew Research Center, *U.S. Muslims Concerned About Their Place in Society, but Continue to Believe in the American Dream*, 26 July 2017. https://www.pewresearch.org/religion/2017/07/26/how-the-u-s-general-public-views-muslims-and-islam/.

37 N. Foner and R. Alba, 'Immigrant Religion in the U.S. and Western Europe: Bridge or Barrier to Inclusion?', *International Migration Review* 42, no. 1 (2008), pp. 360–392. https://onlinelibrary.wiley.com/doi/full/10.1111/j.1747-7379.2008.00128.x#b29.

38 B. Gundelach and A. Manatschal, 'Ethnic Diversity, Social Trust and the Moderating Role of Subnational Integration Policy', *Political Studies* 65, no. 2 (2016), pp. 413–431. https://journals.sagepub.com/doi/10.1177/0032321716644613.

39 E. Solomon, 'Suella Braverman's small boats crackdown is performative cruelty at its worst', *The Guardian*, 7 March 2023. https://www.theguardian.com/commentisfree/2023/mar/07/suella-braverman-small-boats-crackdown-illegal-migrants-uk.

40 UK House of Commons, *Illegal Immigration*, Hansard, 13 December 2022. https://hansard.parliament.uk/commons/2022-12-13/debates/DB61C374-16B5-411C-9A29-CC3DCA119EB3/IllegalImmigration.

41 K. Watson, '"You're not welcome here": Australia's Treatment of Disabled Migrants', *BBC News*, 8 July 2024. https://www.bbc.co.uk/news/articles/cyr70ezev2mo.

42 K. Simonsen and T. Widmann, 'When Do Political Parties Moralize? A Cross-National Study of the Use of Moral Language in Political Communication on Immigration', *British Journal of Political Science*

55 (2025). https://www.cambridge.org/core/journals/british-journal-of-political-science/article/when-do-political-parties-moralize-a-crossnational-study-of-the-use-of-moral-language-in-political-communication-on-immigration/ACFEDBCD015BDEEA277CE689D3816E96.

43 M. Guevara and S. Inskeep, 'Departing DHS Secretary Mayorkas Contends He Delivered Border Security in the End', *KNKX*, 15 January 2025. https://www.knkx.org/2025-01-15/departing-dhs-secretary-mayorkas-contends-he-delivered-border-security-in-the-end.

44 National Commission on Terrorist Attacks Upon the United States, 'Entry of the 9/11 Hijackers into the United States', Staff Statement No. 1. 2004. https://govinfo.library.unt.edu/911/staff_statements/staff_statement_1.pdf.

45 Federal Register, *Protecting the Nation from Foreign Terrorist Entry into the United States*, Executive Order 13769, 27 Federal Register 8977 (1 February 2017). https://www.federalregister.gov/documents/2017/02/01/2017-02281/protecting-the-nation-from-foreign-terrorist-entry-into-the-united-states.

46 It is well established that people with disadvantaged backgrounds are more likely to commit crimes, although reasons are more complex than low income directly causing offending. For example, Per-Olof Wikström argues that social disadvantage causes young people to develop a higher crime propensity and puts them in social contexts where crime is less discouraged: P.-O.H. Wikström and K. Treiber, 'Social Disadvantage and Crime: A Criminological Puzzle', *American Behavioral Scientist* 60, no. 10 (2016), pp. 1232–1259. https://journals.sagepub.com/doi/full/10.1177/0002764216643134.

47 B. Bell, F. Fasani and S. Machin, 'Crime and Immigration: Evidence from Large Immigrant Waves', CEP Discussion Paper No. 1237, Centre for Economic Performance, London School of Economics, 2013, ch. 6. https://eprints.lse.ac.uk/59323/1/CEP_Bell_Fasani_Machin_Crime-and-immigration_2013.pdf.

48 J. McCarthy, 'U.S. Approval of Interracial Marriage at New High of 94%', *Gallup*, 10 September 2021. https://news.gallup.com/poll/354638/approval-interracial-marriage-new-high.aspx.

49 Ipsos, 'Attitudes to Race and Inequality in Great Britain', 15 June 2020, https://www.ipsos.com/en-uk/attitudes-race-and-inequality-great-britain.

50 T.F. Hedegaard and C.A. Larsen, 'The Hidden European Consensus on Migrant Selection: A Conjoint Survey Experiment in the

Netherlands, Germany, Sweden, and Denmark', *Acta Politica* 58 (2023), pp. 717–736. https://link.springer.com/article/10.1057/s41269-022-00261-8; S. Denney and C. Green, 'Who Should be Admitted? Conjoint Analysis of South Korean Attitudes toward Immigrants', *Ethnicities* 21, no. 1 (2020), pp. 120–145. https://journals.sagepub.com/doi/full/10.1177/1468796820916609; L.G. Steele, L. Abdelaaty and N. Than, 'Attitudes about Refugees and Immigrants Arriving in the United States: A Conjoint Experiment', *Ethnic and Racial Studies* 46, no. 10 (2023), pp. 2163–2191. https://www.tandfonline.com/doi/full/10.1080/01419870.2022.2159475; A. Findor, M. Hruška, P. Jankovská and M. Pobudová, 'Who Should Be Given an Opportunity to Live in Slovakia? A Conjoint Experiment on Immigration Preferences', *Journal of Immigrant & Refugee Studies* 20, no. 1 (2021), pp. 79–93. https://www.tandfonline.com/doi/full/10.1080/15562948.2021.1902597; D.G. Ward, 'Public Attitudes toward Young Immigrant Men', *American Political Science Review* 113, no. 1 (2018), pp. 264–269. https://www.cambridge.org/core/journals/american-political-science-review/article/public-attitudes-toward-young-immigrant-men/9422A0C5998C5196444582553E4A41E8; V. Donnaloja, 'British Nationals' Preferences Over Who Gets to Be a Citizen According to a Choice-based Conjoint Experiment', *European Sociological Review* 38, no. 2 (2022), pp. 202–218. https://academic.oup.com/esr/article/38/2/202/6350715.

51 T.F. Hedegaard and C.A. Larsen, 'The Hidden European Consensus on Migrant Selection: A Conjoint Survey Experiment in the Netherlands, Germany, Sweden, and Denmark', *Acta Politica* 58 (2023), pp. 717–736. https://link.springer.com/article/10.1057/s41269-022-00261-8; L. Richards, M. Fernández-Reino and S. Blinder, 'UK Public Opinion toward Immigration: Overall Attitudes and Level of Concern', 24 January 2025. https://migrationobservatory.ox.ac.uk/resources/briefings/uk-public-opinion-toward-immigration-overall-attitudes-and-level-of-concern/; B.J. Newman and N. Malhotra, 'Economic Reasoning with a Racial Hue: Is the Immigration Consensus Purely Race Neutral?', *The Journal of Politics* 81, no. 1 (2019). https://www.benjnewman.com/uploads/1/2/2/1/122135844/newman_malhotra_economicreasoningracialhue_jop.pdf.

52 The Policy Institute, King's College London, 'Love Thy Neighbour? Public Trust and Acceptance of the People who Live Alongside Us', April 2023. https://www.kcl.ac.uk/policy-institute/assets/love-thy-neighbour.pdf.

53 E. Kaufmann, 'Why Culture Is More Important Than Skills: Understanding British Public Opinion on Immigration', *British Politics and Policy at LSE*, 30 January 2018. https://blogs.lse.ac.uk/politicsandpolicy/why-culture-is-more-important-than-skills-understanding-british-public-opinion-on-immigration/.

Chapter 3

1 Home Office, *The Statement of Changes in Immigration Rules: Explanatory Memorandum*, HC1919 (UK Government, March 2019).
2 Home Office, 'Tier 1 Investor Visa route closes over security concerns', 17 February 2022, https://www.gov.uk/government/news/tier-1-investor-visa-route-closes-over-security-concerns.
3 M. Sumption, 'Can Investor Visas Be Made to Work? Lessons from the United Kingdom and United States', University of Oxford, 2024. https://papers.ssrn.com/sol3/papers.cfm?abstract_id=5155988.
4 'Cai Mingjie', *Wikipedia* [last modified 20 January 2024]. https://en.wikipedia.org/wiki/Cai_Mingjie.
5 J. Elrick, *Making Middle-class Multiculturalism* (University of Toronto Press, 2021), p. 99.
6 D.J. DeVoretz, *Canadian Migration Legislation, Policies and Practices* (Advisory Council on Science and Technology, 1999). https://publications.gc.ca/collections/collection_2021/isde-ised/c21-36/C21-36-5-2000-eng.pdf.
7 Department of Home Affairs, *Review of the Points Test: Discussion Paper* (Australian Government, April 2024). https://www.homeaffairs.gov.au/reports-and-pubs/PDFs/points-test-discussion-paper-april-2024.pdf.
8 G.S. Becker, 'The Challenge of Immigration: A Radical Solution', Institute of Economic Affairs, 13 April 2011. https://iea.org.uk/publications/research/the-challenge-of-immigration-a-radical-solution.
9 The Royal Society, *Summary of Visa Costs Analysis (2024)* (Royal Society, August 2024). https://royalsociety.org/-/media/policy/publications/2024/summary-of-visa-costs-analysis-2024.pdf.
10 R. d'Aiglepierre, A. David, C. Levionnois, G. Spielvogel, M. Tuccio and E. Vickstrom, 'A Global Profile of Emigrants to OECD Countries: Younger and More Skilled Migrants from More Diverse Countries', OECD Social, Employment and Migration Working Papers, No. 239, February 2020. https://www.oecd.org/content/dam/oecd/en/publications/reports/2020/02/a-global-profile-of-emigrants-to-oecd-countries_d3315ad9/0cb305d3-en.pdf.

NOTES

11 D.H. McCormick, 'America Needs Smart Immigration Reforms to Win the Race for Global Talent', *Fortune*, 19 February 2021. https://fortune.com/2021/02/19/immigration-reform-biden-us-global-talent-race/.

12 Migration Advisory Committee, 'Impact of international students in the UK' Migration Advisory Committee', 2018. https://www.gov.uk/government/publications/migration-advisory-committee-mac-report-international-students.

13 D.G. Papademetriou, W. Somerville and H. Tanaka, 'Talent in the 21st Century', Migration Policy Institute, 2008. https://www.migrationpolicy.org/research/talent-21st-century-economy.

14 B. Bhardwaj and D. Sharma, 'Migration of Skilled Professionals across the Border: Brain Drain or Brain Gain?', *European Management Journal* 41, no. 6 (2023), pp. 1021–1033. https://www.sciencedirect.com/science/article/abs/pii/S0263237322001773.

15 World Health Organization, *Health Workforce Support and Safeguards List 2023*. https://cdn.who.int/media/docs/default-source/health-workforce/hwf-support-and-safeguards-list8jan.pdf?sfvrsn=1a16bc6f_14&download=true.

16 A. Kamarulzaman, K. Ramnarayan and A.O. Mocumbi, 'Plugging the Medical Brain Drain', *The Lancet* 400, no. 10362 (2022), pp. 1492–1494. https://www.thelancet.com/journals/lancet/article/PIIS0140-6736(22)02087-6/fulltext; D. Schwefel, 'International Health in a Globalized Development Perspective', *Zeitschrift fur Gesundheitswissenschaften* 12, no. 3 (2004), pp. 177–184. https://pmc.ncbi.nlm.nih.gov/articles/PMC7088248/#.

17 E.J. Mills, S. Kanter, A. Hagopian, N. Bansback, J. Nachega, M. Alberton, et al, 'The Financial Cost of Doctors Emigrating from Sub-Saharan Africa: Human Capital Analysis', *BMJ* 343 (2011). https://www.bmj.com/content/343/bmj.d7031.

18 M. Prato, 'The Global Race for Talent: Brain Drain, Knowledge Transfer, and Growth', *The Quarterly Journal of Economics* 140, no. 1 (2025), pp. 165–238. https://academic.oup.com/qje/article/140/1/165/7912563.

19 World Bank, 'World Development Estimates'. https://databank.worldbank.org/source/world-development-indicators/Series/BX.TRF.PWKR.DT.GD.ZS#.

20 N. Cha'Ngom, C. Deuster, F. Docquier and J. Machado, 'Selective Migration and Economic Development: A Generalized Approach', IZA Discussion Paper No. 16222, Institute of Labor Economics, June 2023. https://docs.iza.org/dp16222.pdf.

21 P. Abarcar and C. Theoharides, 'Medical Worker and Origin-Country Human Capital: Evidence from U.S. Visa Policy', *The Review of Economics and Statistics* 106, no. 1 (2024), pp. 20–35. https://direct.mit.edu/rest/article-abstract/106/1/20/107668/Medical-Worker-Migration-and-Origin-Country-Human.

22 L.E. Masselink and S.-Y.D. Lee, 'Government Officials' Representation of Nurses and Migration in the Philippines', *Health Policy and Planning* 28, no. 1 (2013), pp. 90–99. https://pubmed.ncbi.nlm.nih.gov/22437505/.

23 L.K. Bosire, 'Advice to Africans: We Need to Retire the Idea of Brain Drain', *The Africa Report*, 1 February 2021. https://www.theafricareport.com/62649/the-idea-of-african-brain-drain-is-harmful-lets-retire-it/.

24 J.N. Bhagwati, 'Taxing the Brain Drain', *Challenge* 19, no. 3 (1976), pp. 34–38. https://www.jstor.org/stable/40719435?seq=1.

Chapter 4

1 Migration Advisory Committee (MAC), *EEA Migration in the UK: Final Report*, September 2018, p. 120. https://assets.publishing.service.gov.uk/media/5ba26c1de5274a54d5c39be2/Final_EEA_report.PDF.

2 T. Frattini, *The Impact of Migration on UK Consumer Prices*, January 2014. https://assets.publishing.service.gov.uk/media/5a7db5f240f0b65d8b4e3075/Impact_of_migration_on_UK_consumer_prices__2014.pdf; M. Smolka, 'Exploring the Effect of Immigration on Consumer Prices in Spain', CESifo Working Paper No. 11097, 2024. https://papers.ssrn.com/sol3/papers.cfm?abstract_id=4820844.

3 P. Cortes and J. Tessada, 'Low-Skilled Immigration and the Labor Supply of Highly Skilled Women', *American Economic Journal: Applied Economics* 3, no. 3 (2011), pp. 88–123. https://www.jstor.org/stable/41288640?seq=1.

4 E. Lewis, 'Immigration, Skill Mix, and Capital Skill Complementarity', *The Quarterly Journal of Economics* 126, no. 2 (2011), pp. 1029–1069. https://academic.oup.com/qje/article-abstract/126/2/1029/1869919.

5 U.S. Government Accountability Office (GAO), 'H-2A Visa Program: Agencies Should Take Additional Steps to Improve Oversight and Enforcement', 2024. https://www.gao.gov/assets/gao-25-106389.pdf; Centro de los Derechos del Migrante, Inc.,

'Ripe for Reform: Abuse of Agricultural Workers in the H-2A Visa Program', 2020. https://cdmigrante.org/ripe-for-reform/.
6. M. Ruhs, *The Price of Rights: Regulating International Labor Migration* (Princeton University Press, 2013).
7. D. Hiebert, 'Understanding the Impact of Immigration on Demography: A Canadian Case Study', Migration Policy Institute, 2025. https://www.migrationpolicy.org/sites/default/files/publications/mpi-tcm_canada-demographics-immigration-2025_final.pdf.
8. Office for National Statistics (ONS), 'Living Longer and Old-Age Dependency: What Does the Future Hold?', 24 June 2019. https://www.ons.gov.uk/peoplepopulationandcommunity/births deathsandmarriages/ageing/articles/livinglongerandoldage dependencywhatdoesthefuturehold/2019-06-24; Adviesraad Migratie, 'Verkenning Arbeidsmigratie: Oplossing voor Economie en Demografie', 2023. https://www.adviesraadmigratie.nl/publicaties/publicaties/2023/12/11/verkenning-arbeidsmigratie-oplossing-voor-economie-en-demografie.
9. E. Glaeser, *Agglomeration Economics* (Chicago University Press, 2010).
10. I'm grateful to Mark Hofman for pointing this out to me years ago, well before this point became part of the mainstream debate about the economics of immigration.
11. J. Hainmueller and D.J. Hopkins, 'The Hidden American Immigration Consensus: A Conjoint Analysis of Attitudes Toward Immigrants', *American Journal of Political Science* 59, no. 3 (2015), pp. 529–548. https://doi.org/10.1111/ajps.2015.59.issue-3; M. Helbling and H. Kriesi, 'Why Citizens Prefer High- Over Low-Skilled Immigrants: Labor Market Competition, Welfare State, and Deservingness', *European Sociological Review* 30, no. 5 (2014), pp. 595–614. https://academic.oup.com/esr/article-abstract/30/5/595/2763449.
12. A. Kustov, *In Our Interest: How Democracies Can Make Immigration Popular* (Columbia University Press, 2025).
13. Ipsos & British Future, 'Attitudes towards Immigration', 2023. https://www.ipsos.com/sites/default/files/ct/news/documents/2023-09/unbound-british-future-immigration-tracker-2023-charts.pdf.
14. C. Cooper, S. Mulley and W. Somerville, 'Migration in the Age of Insecurity', 2024, p. 26. https://www.labourtogether.uk/all-reports/migration-in-the-age-of-insecurity.

15 T. Burke and A. Giles, 'Visa Reform Targets the Skills Australia Needs', *Ministers' Media Centre*, 2024. https://ministers.dewr.gov.au/burke/visa-reform-targets-skills-australia-needs.

Chapter 5

1. S. Bonjour, 'Family Norms in Migration Politics', 2022. https://www.youtube.com/watch?v=cqsog6NCmnQ.
2. Ibid.
3. D. Miller, *Strangers in Our Midst: The Political Philosophy of Immigration* (Harvard University Press, 2016); J. Carens, *The Ethics of Immigration* (Oxford University Press, 2013).
4. S. Bonjour, 'The Power and Morals of Policymakers: Reassessing the Control Gap Debate', *International Migration Review* 45, no. 1 (2011), pp. 89–122; C. Joppke, 'Why Liberal States Accept Unwanted Immigration', *World Politics* 50, no. 2 (1998), pp. 266–293.
5. S.W. Goodman, 'Integration Requirements for Integration's Sake? Identifying, Categorising and Comparing Civic Integration Policies', *Journal of Ethnic and Migration Studies* 36, no. 5 (2010), pp. 753–772. https://www.tandfonline.com/doi/full/10.1080/13691831003764300#d1e395.
6. OECD, 'International Migration Outlook 2023', 2023. https://www.oecd.org/en/publications/international-migration-outlook-2023_b0f40584-en.html.
7. Eurostat, 'Main Characteristics of Foreign-born People on the Labour Market', 2022. https://ec.europa.eu/eurostat/statistics-explained/index.php?title=Main_characteristics_of_foreign-born_people_on_the_labour_market.
8. Migration Advisory Committee, 'Family Visa Financial Requirements Review (Accessible)', 2025. https://www.gov.uk/government/publications/family-visa-financial-requirements-review/family-visa-financial-requirements-review-accessible.
9. D. Taylor, 'UK Visa Income Test "Cruel" Barrier to Family Reunions, Says Charity', *The Guardian*, 22 December 2024. https://www.theguardian.com/world/2024/dec/22/children-are-hidden-victims-of-immigration-rules-that-separate-families.
10. Immigration Services Department, The United Republic of Tanzania, 'Dependent Pass'. https://immigration.go.tz/index.php/dependent-pass.
11. Migration Advisory Committee, 'Family Visa Financial Requirements Review (Accessible)', 2025. https://www.gov.uk/

government/publications/family-visa-financial-requirements-review/family-visa-financial-requirements-review-accessible.

12 Annie E. Casey Foundation, 'Child Well-being in Single-parent Families', 2024. https://www.aecf.org/blog/child-well-being-in-single-parent-families.

13 Children's Legal Centre, 'Children: The Hidden Victims of Harsh Minimum Income Requirements for Non-British Partners', 2024. https://childrenslegalcentre.com/children-hidden-victims-harsh-minimum-income-requirements/.

14 K. Charsley, 'Risk and Ritual: The Protection of British Pakistani Women in Transnational Marriage', *Journal of Ethnic and Migration Studies* 32, no. 7 (2006), pp. 1169–1187. https://www.tandfonline.com/doi/full/10.1080/13691830600821877#d1e570.

15 S. Carol, E. Ersanilli and M. Wagner, 'Spousal Choice among the Children of Turkish and Moroccan Immigrants in Six European Countries: Transnational Spouse or Co-ethnic Migrant?', *International Migration Review* 48, no. 2 (2014), pp. 387–414.

16 A. Kanas and S. Steinmetz, 'Economic Outcomes of Immigrants with Different Migration Motives: The Role of Labour Market Policies', *European Sociological Review* 37, no. 3 (2021), pp. 449–464. https://academic.oup.com/esr/article-abstract/37/3/449/5999096.

17 E. Ortiz-Ospina, B. Rohenkohl, P. Arriagada and M. Roser, 'Government Spending', *Our World in Data*, October 2016. https://ourworldindata.org/government-spending.

18 C. Bertram, 'Basic Rights, Membership and the UK's Toxic Immigration Debate', *Crooked Timber*, 21 May 2014. https://crookedtimber.org/2014/05/21/basic-rights-membership-and-the-uks-toxic-immigration-debate/.

19 Office for National Statistics (ONS), 'Earnings and Employment from Pay As You Earn Real Time Information, Seasonally Adjusted', 17 July 2025. (Includes both part-time and full-time jobs.) https://www.ons.gov.uk/employmentandlabourmarket/peopleinwork/earningsandworkinghours/datasets/realtimeinformationstatisticsreferencetableseasonallyadjusted.

20 Caroline Coombs is the executive director of Reunite Families UK, an advocacy group.

21 Richmond Kwame Djaou v. Secretary of State for the Home Department, UI-2024-001760 (2025). https://tribunalsdecisions.service.gov.uk/utiac/ui-2024-001760.

22 E. Beck-Gernsheim, 'Transnational Lives, Transnational Marriages: A Review of the Evidence from Migrant Communities in

Europe', *Global Networks* 7, no. 3 (2007), pp. 271–288. https://onlinelibrary.wiley.com/doi/abs/10.1111/j.1471-0374.2007.00169.x; S. Carol, E. Ersanilli and M. Wagner, 'Spousal Choice among the Children of Turkish and Moroccan Immigrants in Six European Countries: Transnational Spouse or Co-ethnic Migrant?', *International Migration Review* 48, no. 2 (2018), pp. 387–414. https://journals.sagepub.com/doi/10.1111/imre.12068?icid=int.sj-abstract.citing-articles.42.

23   R. Pande, 'Becoming Modern: British-Indian Discourses of Arranged Marriages', *Social & Cultural Geography* 17, no. 3 (2016), pp. 380–400.

24   L. Block, '"(Im-)proper" Members with "(Im-)proper" Families? Framing Spousal Migration Policies in Germany', *Journal of Ethnic and Migration Studies* 47, no. 2 (2019), pp. 379–396. https://www.tandfonline.com/doi/full/10.1080/1369183X.2019.1625132.

25   Secretary of State for the Home Department, 'Secure Borders, Safe Haven: Integration with Diversity in Modern Britain', 2002. https://assets.publishing.service.gov.uk/government/uploads/system/uploads/attachment_data/file/250926/cm5387.pdf.

26   S. Balgamwalla, 'Bride and Prejudice: How US Immigration Law Discriminates Against Spousal Visa Holders', *Berkeley Journal of Gender, Law & Justice* 29, no. 1 (2014), pp. 25–71. https://papers.ssrn.com/sol3/papers.cfm?abstract_id=2235858.

27   M. Rytter, '"The Family of Denmark" and "the Aliens": Kinship Images in Danish Integration Politics', *Ethnos: Journal of Anthropology* 75, no. 3 (2010), pp. 301–322. https://pure.au.dk/ws/files/74697221/Ethnos_Rytter2010.pdf.

28   Court of Justice of the European Union, *Case C-89/18, A, ECLI:EU:C:2019:580*, 10 July 2019. https://curia.europa.eu/juris/document/document.jsf?docid=216036&text=&dir=&doclang=EN&part=1&occ=first&mode=DOC&pageIndex=0&cid=6037047.

29   C.J. McKinney and M. Sumption, 'Migrants on Ten-year Routes to Settlement in the UK', The Migration Observatory, 2021. https://migrationobservatory.ox.ac.uk/resources/briefings/migrants-on-ten-year-routes-to-settlement-in-the-uk/.

30   Office for Budget Responsibility, 'Fiscal Risks and Sustainability – September 2024', 12 September 2024, ch. 4. https://obr.uk/frs/fiscal-risks-and-sustainability-september-2024/.

31   Department of Home Affairs, Australian Government, 'Visa Processing Times'. https://immi.homeaffairs.gov.au/visas/getting-a-visa/visa-processing-times/family-visa-processing-priorities/parent-visas-queue-release-dates.

NOTES

Chapter 6

1. Arton Capital, *Birthright Citizenship in 2025*, 2025. https://www.artoncapital.com/industry-news/countries-offer-birthright-citizenship-in-2025/.
2. BBC, 'Thematic Review of the Impartiality of BBC Content on Migration', Audience Research Report, 2024. https://www.bbc.co.uk/aboutthebbc/documents/thematic-review-migration-audience-research-report-may-2024.pdf.
3. For a review, see J. Barnes, M.M. Naser and J.N. Aston, 'A Vulnerability Approach to Irregular Migration and Modern Slavery in Australia', *Australian Journal of Human Rights* 29, no. 1 (2023), pp. 121–140. https://doi.org/10.1080/1323238X.2023.2229619.
4. E. Alden, 'Is Border Enforcement Effective? What We Know and What It Means', *Journal on Migration and Human Security* 5, no. 2 (2017), pp. 481–490. https://journals.sagepub.com/doi/pdf/10.1177/233150241700500213.
5. A. Bloch, L. Kumarappan and S. Mckay, 'Employer Sanctions: The Impact of Workplace Raids and Fines on Undocumented Migrants and Ethnic Enclave Employers', *Critical Social Policy* 35, no. 1 (2014), pp. 132–151. https://journals.sagepub.com/doi/full/10.1177/0261018314545600; for the United States: P.M. Orrenius, M. Zavodny and C. Smith, 'Labor Market Effects of Worker- and Employer-Targeted Immigration Enforcement', Federal Reserve Bank of Dallas, Working Paper 2413, 2024. https://www.dallasfed.org/-/media/documents/research/papers/2024/wp2413.pdf.
6. A. Vinogradova, 'Illegal Immigration, Deportation Policy, and the Optimal Timing of Return', *Journal of Population Economics* 29 (2016), pp. 781–816. https://link.springer.com/article/10.1007/s00148-016-0586-z; C. Amuedo-Dorantes, T. Puttitanun and A. Martinez-Donate, 'How Do Tougher Immigration Measures Impact Unauthorized Immigrants?', IZA Discussion Paper No. 7134, 2013. https://docs.iza.org/dp7134.pdf.
7. Home Office, *Employer Awareness of, and Self-reported Compliance with, Right to Work Checks*, 1 April 2025. https://www.gov.uk/government/publications/employer-awareness-of-right-to-work-checks/employer-awareness-of-and-self-reported-compliance-with-right-to-work-checks.
8. Pew Research Center, 'What We Know About Unauthorized Immigrants Living in the U.S.', 22 July 2024. https://www.pewresearch.org/short-reads/2024/07/22/what-we-know-about-unauthorized-immigrants-living-in-the-us/.

9   D. Kierans and C. Vargas-Silva, 'The Irregular Migrant Population of Europe', MIrreM Working Paper No. 11/2024, 2024. https://irregularmigration.eu/wp-content/uploads/2024/10/MIRREM-Kierans-and-Vargas-Silva-2024-Irregular-Migrant-Population-in-Europe-v1.pdf.

10   C. Yeo, 'High and Low Resistance Deportations', *We Wanted Workers (Substack)*, 5 March 2025. https://wewantedworkers.substack.com/p/high-and-low-resistance-deportations.

11   Frontex, 'Guide for Joint Return Operations by Air Coordinated by Frontex', European Border and Coast Guard Agency, 2016. https://www.frontex.europa.eu/assets/Publications/General/Guide_for_Joint_Return_Operations_by_Air_coordinated_by_Frontex.pdf; C. Jones, J. Kilpatrick and M. Gkliati, 'Deportation Union: Rights, Accountability, and the EU's Push to Increased Forced Removals', *Statewatch*, 2020. https://www.statewatch.org/media/1321/deportation-union.pdf.

12   J. Gest, M.J. Gigante, N. Kaptanoğlu, I.M. Kysel and L. Núñez, 'Migrant Rights Protections and Their Implementation in 45 Countries', *International Migration Review* (2024). https://journals.sagepub.com/doi/full/10.1177/01979183241278613.

13   C. Bansak and S. Pearlman, 'The Impact of Legalizing Unauthorized Immigrants', *IZA World of Labor* (2021), Article 245. https://wol.iza.org/articles/legalizing-undocumented-immigrants/long.

14   G.J. Borjas and A. Edo, 'Monopsony, Efficiency, and the Regularization of Undocumented Immigrants', NBER Working Paper 31457, 2023. https://www.nber.org/papers/w31457.

15   S.R. Baker, 'Effects of Immigrant Legalization on Crime', *American Economic Review* 105, no. 5 (2015), pp. 210–213. https://www.aeaweb.org/articles?id=10.1257%2Faer.p20151041.

16   C. Bansak and S. Pearlman, 'The Impact of Legalizing Unauthorized Immigrants', *IZA World of Labor* (2021), Article 245. https://wol.iza.org/articles/legalizing-undocumented-immigrants/long; O. Marie and P. Pinotti, 'Immigration and Crime: An International Perspective', *Journal of Economic Perspectives* 38, no. 1 (2024), pp. 181–200. https://pubs.aeaweb.org/doi/pdfplus/10.1257/jep.38.1.181; J. Portes and M. Ventura-Arrieta, 'The Impact of Regularisation', Citizens UK, 2022. https://citizensuk.contentfiles.net/media/documents/Settle_Our_Status_-_Impact_of_Regularisation.pdf; I. Galvez-Iniesta, 'The Size, Socioeconomic Composition and Fiscal Implications of the Irregular Immigration

in Spain', Working Paper, 2020-08, 2020. https://e-archivo.uc3m. es/rest/api/core/bitstreams/1f19ed21-ac46-4007-9637-bd60e73bbc19/ content.
17 T.L. Bah and C. Batista, 'Understanding Willingness to Migrate Illegally: Evidence from a Lab in the Field Experiment', NOVAFRICA Working Paper No. 1803, 2018. https://research.unl. pt/ws/portalfiles/portal/26451092/Understanding_willingness_to_ migrate_illegally_wp.pdf.
18 P.M. Orrenius and M. Zavodny, 'Do Amnesty Programs Reduce Undocumented Immigration? Evidence from Irca', *Demography* 40 (2003), pp. 437–450. https://link.springer.com/article/10.1353/ dem.2003.0028.
19 F. Wehinger, 'Do Amnesties Pull in Illegal Immigrants? An Analysis of European Apprehension Data', *Migration and Border Studies* 1, no. 2 (2014), pp. 231–246. https://www.indersciencelonline.com/ doi/abs/10.1504/IJMBS.2014.066312.
20 Pew Research Center, 'What We Know About Unauthorized Immigrants Living in the U.S.', 22 July 2024. https://www. pewresearch.org/short-reads/2024/07/22/what-we-know-about-unauthorized-immigrants-living-in-the-us/.
21 Akhtar Hussain v. Secretary of State for the Home Department, UI-2024-000981, [2024] UKUT 981 (IAC) (2024). https://tribunals decisions.service.gov.uk/utiac/ui-2024-000981.
22 R. Cooper, 'Legal Pathways' Effects on Irregular Migration', Helpdesk Report, 5 April 2019. https://assets.publishing.service. gov.uk/media/5cd99936e5274a38bed21639/569_Regular_ Pathways_Effects_on_Iregular_Migration.pdf.
23 S. Mukherjee and J.M. Krogstad, 'Trump and Harris Supporters Differ on Mass Deportations but Favor Border Security, High-Skilled Immigration', Pew Research Center, 27 September 2024. https://www.pewresearch.org/race-and-ethnicity/2024/09/27/ trump-and-harris-supporters-differ-on-mass-deportations-but-favor-border-security-high-skilled-immigration/.
24 L. Gschwind, M. Ruhs, A. Ahlen and J. Palme, 'Public Preferences for Policies vis-à-vis Irregular Migrants in Europe: The Roles of Policy Design and Context', PRIME Research Paper, 2025. https://cadmus.eui.eu/entities/publication/d839f90e-2736-581f-84b4-15911fca4c3e/full.

Chapter 7

1. Term coined by J. Hathaway, 'Forced Migration Studies: Could We Agree Just to "Date"?', *Journal of Refugee Studies* 20, no. 3 (2007), pp. 349–369. https://academic.oup.com/jrs/article/20/3/349/1591558.
2. D.S. FitzGerald, *Refuge Beyond Reach: How Rich Democracies Repel Asylum Seekers* (Oxford University Press, 2019).
3. Eurostat, 'Asylum and First Time Asylum Applicants by Citizenship, Age and Sex – Quarterly Data (Table Code: migr_asydcfstq)', European Commission. https://ec.europa.eu/eurostat/databrowser/view/migr_asydcfstq/default/table.
4. Freedom from Torture, 'Beyond Belief: How the Home Office Fails Survivors of Torture at the Asylum Interview', 2020. https://beyondbelief.freedomfromtorture.org/media/files/Beyond-Belief.pdf.
5. A. Vogl, 'Introduction', *Judging Refugees: Narrative and Oral Testimony in Refugee Status Determination* (Cambridge University Press, 2024), pp. 1–22. https://www.cambridge.org/core/books/judging-refugees/introduction/FB61D4F6C6733A85A22812E2E7E2BE66
6. See, for example, J. Hyde, 'SRA Charges Two More Solicitors after Immigration Sting', *Law Gazette*, 12 September 2024. https://www.lawgazette.co.uk/news/sra-charges-two-more-solicitors-after-immigration-sting/5120825.article; Canada Border Services Agency, 'CBSA Cracks Down on Fraudulent Refugee Claims', News Release, 1 October 2020. https://www.canada.ca/en/border-services-agency/news/2020/10/cbsa-cracks-down-on-fraudulent-refugee-claims.html/
7. Eurostat, 'Final Decisions in Appeal or Review on Applications by Type of Decision, Citizenship, Age and Sex – Annual Data (Table Code: migr_asydcfina)', European Commission. https://ec.europa.eu/eurostat/databrowser/view/migr_asydcfina/default/table.
8. Transactional Records Access Clearinghouse (TRAC), 'Immigration Judges: Report on Asylum Decisions in 2023', Syracuse University, 2024. https://trac.syr.edu/immigration/reports/judge2023/.
9. Eurostat, 'Temporary Protection for Persons Fleeing Ukraine – Monthly Statistics', European Commission, 2025. https://ec.europa.eu/eurostat/statistics-explained/index.php?title=Temporary_protection_for_persons_fleeing_Ukraine_-_monthly_statistics.
10. M. Marbach, J. Hainmueller and D. Hangartner, 'The Long-term Impact of Employment Bans on the Economic Integration of Refugees', *Science Advances* 4 (2018). https://www.science.org/doi/10.1126/sciadv.aap9519.

NOTES

11 UNHCR (United Nations High Commissioner for Refugees), *Mid-Year Trends 2023* (UNHCR, 2024). https://www.unhcr.org/mid-year-trends.

12 T. Ginn, R. Resstack, H. Dempster, E. Arnold-Fernández, S. Miller, M. Guerrero Ble and B. Kanyamanza, *2022 Global Refugee Work Rights Report* (Center for Global Development, 2022). https://www.cgdev.org/sites/default/files/2022-global-refugee-work-rights-report.pdf.

13 A. Betts and P. Collier, *Refuge: Transforming a Broken Refugee System* (Allen Lane, 2017), p. 107.

14 G. Restelli, 'Does Aid to Migrants in "Transit Countries" Affect their Movement Intentions? Evidence from Libya', *World Development* 191 (2025), Article 106980. https://www.sciencedirect.com/science/article/pii/S0305750X25000658#b22.

15 Chatham House, 'Why Aren't Gulf Countries Taking Syrian Refugees?', September 2015. https://www.chathamhouse.org/2015/09/why-arent-gulf-countries-taking-syrian-refugees.

16 L. Detlefsen, T. Heidland and C. Schneiderheinze, 'What Explains People's Migration Aspirations? Experimental Evidence from Sub-Saharan Africa', 5 October 2022. https://ssrn.com/abstract=4238957.

17 UNHCR, *Global Trends: Forced Displacement in 2023* (UNHCR, 2024). https://www.unhcr.org/global-trends-report-2023.

18 P. Walsh and N. Jorgensen, 'Asylum and Refugee Resettlement in the UK', Migration Observatory, 2025. https://migrationobservatory.ox.ac.uk/resources/briefings/migration-to-the-uk-asylum/.

19 A.-M. Jeannet, E. Ademmer, M. Ruhs and T. Stöhr, 'What Asylum and Refugee Policies do Europeans Want? Evidence from a Cross-national Conjoint Experiment', European University Institute, RSCAS 2019/73. https://cadmus.eui.eu/bitstream/handle/1814/64384/RSCAS_2019_73.pdf.

20 D.S. FitzGerald, *Refuge Beyond Reach: How Rich Democracies Repel Asylum Seekers* (Oxford University Press, 2019).

21 M. Barslund, M. Busse, K. Lenaerts, L. Ludolph and V. Renman, 'Integration of Refugees: Lessons from Bosnians in Five EU Countries', *Intereconomics* 52, no. 5 (2017), pp. 257–263. https://www.intereconomics.eu/contents/year/2017/number/5/article/integration-of-refugees-lessons-from-bosnians-in-five-eu-countries.html.

22 OECD, *International Migration Outlook 2021* (OECD, 2021), ch. 4.

23 Z. Kone, I. Ruiz and C. Vargas-Silva, 'Refugees and the UK Labour Market', *COMPAS*, 2019. https://www.compas.ox.ac.uk/wp-content/uploads/ECONREF-Refugees-and-the-UK-Labour-Market-report.pdf; W. Evans and D. Fitzgerald, 'The Economic and Social Outcomes of Refugees in the United States: Evidence from the ACS', NBER Working Paper No. 23498, National Bureau of Economic Research, 2017. https://www.nber.org/system/files/working_papers/w23498/w23498.pdf.

24 J. van de Beek, J. Hartog, G. Kreffer and H. Roodenburg, 'The Long-Term Fiscal Impact of Immigrants in the Netherlands, Differentiated by Motive, Source Region and Generation', IZA Discussion Papers, No. 17569, 2024. https://docs.iza.org/dp17569.pdf.

25 P. Varela, N. Husek, T. Williams, R. Maher and D. Kennedy, 'The Lifetime Fiscal Impact of the Australian Permanent Migration Program', Treasury Working Paper, 2021. https://treasury.gov.au/sites/default/files/2021-12/p2021-220773_1.pdf.

26 H. Zhang, J. Zhong and C. de Chardon, 'Immigrants' Net Direct Fiscal Contribution: How Does It Change Over Their Lifetime?', *Canadian Journal of Economics/Revue canadienne d'économique* 53, no. 4 (2020), pp. 1642–1662. https://onlinelibrary.wiley.com/doi/full/10.1111/caje.12477.

27 W. Evans and D. Fitzgerald, 'The Economic and Social Outcomes of Refugees in the United States: Evidence from the ACS', NBER Working Paper No. 23498, National Bureau of Economic Research, 2017. https://www.nber.org/system/files/working_papers/w23498/w23498.pdf.

28 See, for example, European Court of Human Rights (ECtHR), *M.S.S. v. Belgium and Greece* [GC], Application No. 30696/09. Judgment of January 21, 2011. https://www.asylumlawdatabase.eu/en/content/ecthr-mss-v-belgium-and-greece-gc-application-no-3069609.

29 Immigration, Refugees and Citizenship Canada (IRCC), 'Asylum Claims by Year', Government of Canada. https://open.canada.ca/data/en/dataset/b6cbcf4d-f763-4924-a2fb-8cc4a06e3de4/resource/63f3ba24-cb8d-4c27-9c3d-3b53b9a9dfcc.

30 P. Walsh and M. Sumption, 'UK Policies to Deter People from Claiming Asylum', Migration Observatory, 2024. https://migrationobservatory.ox.ac.uk/resources/commentaries/uk-policies-to-deter-people-from-claiming-asylum/.

NOTES

31 A. Fiedler, 'From Being Aware to Going There: On the Awareness and Decision-making of (Prospective) Migrants', *Mass Communication and Society* 23, no. 3 (2020), pp. 356–377. https://www.tandfonline.com/doi/full/10.1080/15205436.2019.1666992.

32 L. Mbaye, '"Barcelona or Die": Understanding Illegal Migration from Senegal', *IZA Journal of Migration* 3, no. 21 (2014). https://doi.org/10.1186/s40176-014-0021-8.

33 T. Bah and C. Batista, 'Understanding Willingness to Migrate Illegally: Evidence from a Lab in the Field Experiment', Nova Africa Working Paper Series Working Paper No 1803, revised June 2020. https://research.unl.pt/ws/portalfiles/portal/26451092/Understanding_willingness_to_migrate_illegally_wp.pdf.

34 L. Detlefsen, T. Heidland and C. Schneiderheinze, 'What Explains People's Migration Aspirations? Experimental Evidence from Sub-Saharan Africa', 5 October 2022. https://ssrn.com/abstract=4238957.

35 See, for example, A. Pronk, 'The Price of Deterrence: Australia's Path to Maintaining Sovereign Borders', Clingendael, February 2024. https://www.clingendael.org/sites/default/files/2024-02/Clingendael_Report_In_Search_of_Control_Australia.pdf.

36 Refugee Council of Australia, 'How Many People Has Australia Sent Offshore? Where Are They Now?'. https://www.refugeecouncil.org.au/operation-sovereign-borders-offshore-detention-statistics/2/

37 N. Welfens and S. Bonjour, 'Families First? The Mobilization of Family Norms in Refugee Resettlement', *International Political Sociology* 15, no. 2 (2021), pp. 212–231. https://academic.oup.com/ips/article/15/2/212/5959724.

38 N. Welfens, '"Promising Victimhood": Contrasting Deservingness Requirements in Refugee Resettlement', *Journal of Ethnic and Migration Studies* 49, no. 5 (2023), pp. 1103–1124. https://www.tandfonline.com/doi/full/10.1080/1369183X.2022.2117686#d1e139.

39 L. Detlefsen, T. Heidland and C. Schneiderheinze, 'What Explains People's Migration Aspirations? Experimental Evidence from Sub-Saharan Africa', 5 October 2022. https://ssrn.com/abstract=4238957.

40 Home Office, 'Ukraine Family Scheme, Ukraine Sponsorship Scheme (Homes for Ukraine) and Ukraine Extension Scheme Visa Data', updated 19 December 2024. https://www.gov.uk/government/publications/ukraine-family-scheme-application-data/ukraine-family-scheme-and-ukraine-sponsorship-scheme-homes-for-ukraine-visa-data--2

41 P. Walsh and N. Jorgensen, 'Asylum and Refugee Resettlement in the UK', Migration Observatory, 2024. https://migrationobservatory.ox.ac.uk/resources/briefings/migration-to-the-uk-asylum/.

42 U.S. Department of Homeland Security Office of the Inspector General, 'CBP Did Not Thoroughly Plan for CBP One™ Risks, and Opportunities to Implement Improvements Exist', DHS, 2024. https://www.oig.dhs.gov/sites/default/files/assets/2024-08/OIG-24-48-Aug24.pdf.

43 U.S. Customs and Border Protection, 'CBP Releases December 2024 Monthly Update', 14 January 2025. https://www.cbp.gov/newsroom/national-media-release/cbp-releases-december-2024-monthly-update.

44 M. Clemens, 'The Effect of Lawful Crossing on Unlawful Crossing at the US Southwest Border', Peterson Institute for International Economics, Working Paper 24-10. https://www.piie.com/publications/working-papers/2024/effect-lawful-crossing-unlawful-crossing-us-southwest-border.

45 C. Putzel-Kavanaugh and A.G. Ruiz Soto, 'With New Strategies at and Beyond the U.S. Border, Migrant Encounters Plunge', Migration Policy Institute, October 2024. https://www.migrationpolicy.org/news/fy2024-us-border-encounters-plunge.

46 S. Fratzke, M. Benton and A. Selee, 'Legal Pathways and Enforcement: What the U.S. Safe Mobility Strategy Can Teach Europe about Migration Management', Migration Policy Institute, 2024. https://www.migrationpolicy.org/news/lessons-us-safe-mobility-strategy-europe

47 D.S. FitzGerald, *Refuge Beyond Reach: How Rich Democracies Repel Asylum Seekers* (Oxford University Press, 2019).

48 S. Reynolds and J.P. Vacatello, 'Building a Lifeline: A Proposed Global Platform and Responsibility Sharing Model for the Global Compact on Refugees', *Scholar* 21 (2019), p. 325.

49 A. Betts and P. Collier, *Refuge: Transforming a Broken Refugee System* (Allen Lane, 2017).

Chapter 8

1 P. DeLeon, 'Public Policy Termination: An End and a Beginning', *Policy Analysis* (1978), pp. 369–392.

2 Our World in Data, 'Share of the Population that were born in another country', Our World in Data, 2025. https://ourworldindata.org/grapher/migrant-stock-share?tab=chart.

NOTES

3   Kantar Public and Migration Observatory, 'Public Attitudes Towards Immigration', Kantar Public, June 2023. https://kantar.turtl.co/story/public-attitudes-to-immigration/page/1.

4   M. Georgiou and R. Zaborowski, *Media Coverage of the 'Refugee Crisis': A Cross-European Perspective* (Council of Europe, 2017). https://edoc.coe.int/en/refugees/7367-media-coverage-of-the-refugee-crisis-a-cross-european-perspective.html

5   Migration Observatory, 'Off Target: Government Policies Are Not on Track to Reducing Net Migration to the Tens of Thousands by 2015', Migration Observatory, University of Oxford, 2011. https://migrationobservatory.ox.ac.uk/resources/commentaries/off-target-government-policies-are-not-on-track-to-reducing-net-migration-to-the-tens-of-thousands-by-2015/.

6   A. Kustov and M. Landgrave, 'Immigration Is Difficult?! Informing Voters about Immigration Policy Fosters pro-Immigration Views', *Journal of Experimental Political Science* (2025), pp. 1–13. https://doi.org/10.1017/XPS.2024.21. https://www.cambridge.org/core/journals/journal-of-experimental-political-science/article/immigration-is-difficult-informing-voters-about-immigration-policy-fosters-proimmigration-views/464D2A994E38A25EE49B1464C6729773. See also E. Thorson and L. Abdelaaty, 'Misperceptions about Refugee Policy', *American Political Science Review* 117, no. 3 (2023), pp. 1123–1129. https://doi.org/10.1017/S0003055422000910.

7   P. Conzo, G. Fuochi, L. Anfossi, F. Spaccatini and C.O. Mosso, 'Negative Media Portrayals of Immigrants Increase Ingroup Favoritism and Hostile Physiological and Emotional Reactions', *Scientific Reports* 11, no. 1 (2021), Article 16407. https://www.nature.com/articles/s41598-021-95800-2; M. Sagir and S.T. Mockabee, 'Public Attitudes toward Immigration: Was There a Trump Effect?', *American Politics Research* 51, no. 3 (2023), pp. 381–396. https://journals.sagepub.com/doi/10.1177/1532673X221139762.

8   A. Kustov, *In Our Interest: How Democracies Can Make Immigration Popular* (Columbia University Press, 2025).

9   M. Helbling, R. Maxwell and R. Traunmüller, 'Numbers, Selectivity, and Rights: The Conditional Nature of Immigration Policy Preferences', *Comparative Political Studies* 57, no. 2 (2024), pp. 254–286. https://journals.sagepub.com/doi/full/10.1177/00104140231178737.

10 K. Schulz, *Being Wrong* (Granta Books, 2011).

FURTHER READING

For contrasting perspectives on the ethics of immigration, see David Miller, *Strangers in Our Midst: The Political Philosophy of Immigration* (Harvard University Press, 2016) and Joseph Carens, *The Ethics of Immigration* (Oxford University Press, 2013). For an entertaining, radical economic perspective that will unsettle migration liberals and sceptics alike, see Bryan Caplan and Zach Weinersmith's graphic novel, *Open Borders: The Science and Ethics of Immigration* (St Martin's Press, 2019).

On the economics of migration, see Alan Manning, *Why Immigration Policy Is Hard and How to Make It Better* (Polity Press, 2025) and Martin Ruhs, *The Price of Rights: Regulating International Labor Migration* (Princeton University Press, 2013).

On asylum and the Refugee Convention, see David Scott FitzGerald, *Refuge Beyond Reach: How Rich Democracies Repel Asylum Seekers* (Oxford University Press, 2020). For a sceptical perspective on the role of human rights law in immigration policy, see John Finnis and Simon Murray, *Immigration, Strasbourg and Judicial Overreach* (Policy Exchange, 2021).

FURTHER READING

On public opinion and the politics of immigration, see Robert Ford and Matthew Goodwin, *Revolt on the Right: Explaining Support for the Radical Right in Britain* (Routledge, 2014) and Alexander Kustov, *In Our Interest: How Democracies Can Make Immigration Popular* (Columbia University Press, 2025).

To understand liberal and sceptical perspectives on migration, respectively, see Colin Yeo, *Welcome to Britain: Fixing Our Broken Immigration System* (Biteback Publishing, 2022) and David Goodhart, *The British Dream: Successes and Failures of Post-War Immigration* (Atlantic Books Ltd, 2013).

For readers who noted the absence of discussion on citizenship in this volume, Dimitry Kochenov's *Citizenship* (MIT Press, 2019) provides an opinionated but insightful overview.

Information on current UK migration policy and trends is available from the Migration Observatory's website (disclosure: the author of this book is the director): www.migrationobservatory.ox.ac.uk. The Migration Policy Institute publishes reports on a wide range of migration topics, particularly for the United States and Europe: www.migrationpolicy.org. Good sources for global data on migration are the Migration Data Portal (www.migrationdataportal.org) and Our World in Data (https://ourworldindata.org).

INDEX

References to figures are in *italics*; references to tables and boxes are in **bold**.

A

Afghan refugees 133, 135
agricultural sector 15, 19, 21, 59–60, 61, *61*, 65
Algeria 14
Aliens Acts (UK) 5, 6, 44
amnesties 105–107
amnesty *see* legalization
arranged marriages 84–85
asylum seekers *see* refugees and asylum seekers
Australia
    economic approach 159
    investor visas 165
    parent migration 88–89
    partner migration 81
    planned migration 163
    as popular destination **12**
    public opinion *39*
    refugees and asylum 125, 126, 128, 129, **130–131**, *132*, 142, 142–143
    skilled work migrants 166
    visa schemes 32, 46, 47, 48, 70
    'White Australia' policy 36–37
Austria **13**, 46, 111, 124

B

bankers 69
Bataclan terrorist attack 161–162
Becker, Gary 47–49
Belgium **118**
Bertram, Chris 81
birthright citizenship 93
border controls 35, 98, 128–129, 151
Bosire, Lydiah Kemunto 55–56
Bosnian refugees 124
brain drain debate 53–56
Brexit 2, **12–13**

C

Cai Mingjie 44
Canada
    demographic decline **66**, 67–68
    investor visas 165
    'lonely Canadian' rule 77
    partner migration 81
    planned migration 163
    points system 44–45, *46*
    as popular destination 11, **12**
    public opinion *39*
    refugees and asylum 125, 126, 128, 133–134
    skilled work migrants 166

INDEX

Caplan, Bryan 62–63
caps on migration 153
care workers 61, 65, 67, 162
Century Initiative **67–68**
childcare sector 19, 65
Chinese Exclusion Act (US) 6
citizenship tests 1, 30–31
climate migrants **121–122**
closed borders position 13–15
Colombia 14
colonial legacies 9, **14**
compensation **158–159**
constitutional rights 33
Convention Against Torture 115–116
crime 33–36

D

data collection 166–167
demographic decline **66–68**
Denmark 23, 86, 160
deportation 33, 102–104, 110, 115, 124
development funding 41, 56, 120
diversity 23, 24, 27
'Dublin' system 127, 165
Dukach, Semyon 124

E

economic impacts of migration 20–23, 59–60, 62, 80–81, 87–88, 105, 124–125, **158–159**
economics-first strategy 154–155
Ellis Island, New York 1, 7, 75
employer sponsorship 40, 49–50, **63**
employment rates, impact on 20–21
ethical issues 8–15, 16, 31–33, 97, 112–113

Europe
    EU free movement **12–13**, 25, 26, 59–60
    family migration 76
    Mexican migrants **29**
    migrant gender attitudes 25–26, **28**
    Muslim migrants **28–29**
    public opinion 24, 25–26, 111, 123
    public sentiment 161–162
    refugees and asylum 114, **118**, 126, 127, 165
    unauthorized population 101
European Convention on Human Rights (ECHR) 82, 86–87, **108**, 115
European Court of Human Rights 127
exploitation 61, **63**, 95, 100
expression of interest systems 166

F

fairness 31–33
family migration 73–90
    balancing rights 81–82
    economic impacts 80–81, 87–88
    eligibility **77**
    exceptional circumstances **82**–83
    growth of 75–76
    human rights law 82, 86–87
    immigration process 73–74
    incidence of **4**, 76
    income requirements 81–82
    partners 73–74, 76, **77**, 78–86
    parents and other relatives **77**, 87–89
    social and cultural impacts 83–86

fiscal impacts of migration 20, 22, 62, 65, 69, 87, 124–125
foreign policy goals 19
France **12**, **14**, 29, *39*, 128
free movement of people 4, **12–13**, *25*, 59–60
French Revolution 5
Frisch, Max 76

G

generalizations 24–27, 44
Germany **12**, *39*, 84–85, **118**, 165
Giles, Andrew 70
government expenditure statistics 22, 80, 87, 124–125
Greece *39*, 51, 127
Green Card (Peter Weir film) 73
guest workers 76, 109 *see also* seasonal workers

H

health professionals 54, 55
Home Affairs Committee (UK) 42
Honduras 54
hostile environment policies 100–101
housing costs 21, **67**
human rights law 33, 82, 86–87, 103–104, **108**, 114–116
humanitarian approaches 156–158, 156–160

I

illegal migrant, use of term **94**
illegal migration *see* unauthorized migration
Illegal Migration Act 2023 (UK) 139

Immigration Reform and Control Act of 1986 (US) 106
India **14**, 55
industrial revolution 5
integration 23, 27–30, 83–87
interior enforcement 35, 99–102
international agreements 55, 56, 86, 114–115, 137, 141–146
International Organization for Migration 99
international students 51, 55, 56, 162
investor visas 34, 42–43, 165
Iraq 9
Ireland **13**
irregular migrant, use of term **94**
irregular migration *see* unauthorized migration
Italy **12**, *39*, 51, 55, 106, 111, 127

J

Japan **12**, **14**, *39*, 144, 159
Johnson, Boris 162

K

Kurdi, Alan 161
Kustov, Alexander **164**

L

labour migration *see* low-wage work migration; skilled work migration
language tests 30, 36–37
Lebanon 54
liberal views on migration 15–16, 112–113, 167–168
Libya 10
low-migration strategy 150–152, **153**

INDEX

low-wage work migration 58–72
   economic impacts 20–23, 59–60, 62
   employer sponsorship 40, 49–50, **63**
   expendability of 71–72
   non-economic drivers for 64–65, 71
   restrictions on rights 60–64
   seasonal workers 15, 19, 21

M

Matt cartoon 45
May, Theresa 99
Mayorkas, Alejandro 33–34
McCormick, David 51
media coverage 159–160
Mexico 39, 55
Mexican migrants **29**
migrant workers *see* low-wage work migration; skilled work migration
migration statistics 4, **14**
Miller, David 10
moral debates 8–15, 16, 31–33, **97**, 112–113
Morocco 14
Munie, Omar 124
Muslim migrants **28–29**, 35, 84–85, 86

N

national security concerns 33–36
Nepal 54
Netherlands 82, 124–125
New Zealand 32, 46, 166
Nigeria 39, 54
9/11 terrorist attacks 34–35
non-refoulement 115, 122
Norway 39, 166

O

open borders position 8–10, **11–13**, 15, 62–63
opinion polls *see* public opinion

P

Pakistani migrants **28–29**, 79
parent migration 77, 87–89
partner migration 73–74, 76, **77**, 78–86
Patel, Priti 42–43, 112
permanent residence 3, 58, 59, 61, 65, 151, 154, 156, 165
Philippines 39, 55
points systems 44–47
Poland 39, 111
Polish migrants 25
policymakers, use of term **17**
policymaking difficulties and dilemmas 16–17, 18–19, 38–41, 74–75, 91–92, 110, 148–149
political choices 149–150
political competence 165
political persuasion **163–164**
political promises 162–163
population growth **66–68**
Portugal 55
productivity 21–22
public opinion
   changing minds **163–164**
   gender attitudes 25–26
   impact of migration 24
   and middle ground 165
   preferred destinations **11, 12–13**
   preferred types of migrant 37, 68–69
   and racial discrimination 37–38, 39
   refugees and asylum 123

public opinion (continued)
   unauthorized migration 110–111
   understandings of term 'migrant' 3
   wish to migrate **11**
public spending *see* government expenditure statistics
Putin, Vladimir 38
Putnam, Robert 24

R
racial discrimination **29**, 36–38
Rasmussen, Anders 23
Reed, Dr Alfred C. 7
Refugee Convention 114, 120, 122–123, 125, 126–127, 141, 142, 146, 147
refugees and asylum seekers 112–147
   asylum process 116–119
   and climate change **121–122**
   deterrence and enforcement 125–132
   draw of high-income states *4*, 119–120
   economic impacts of 124–125
   gender imbalance **120–121**
   global protection regime 114–119
   migrants distinguished 116, **117–118**
   moral debate 112–113
   offering legal routes 107–110, 132–139
   public opinion 123
   quota system 143–146
   refugee defined 114, 116, **117**
   replacing current system 139–146
   uncontrollability of 122–123
   UNHCR refugee resettlement **121**, 132–133

regularization *see* legalization
remittances 54
removals *see* deportation
'right to work' checks 100, 157
Ruhs, Martin 62, 158
Russia *39*, **118**
Rwanda deal 129–130

S
safe and legal routes 134–139, 145–146, 147, 154
safe third countries 141
Saudi Arabia 12
sceptical views on migration 15–16, 112, 113, 167–168
Schuck, Peter 143–144
seasonal workers 15, 19, 21
Senegal 129
shortage occupation lists **70–71**
Singapore 1, 44, 53, 58
Sivanandan, Ambalavaner **14**
skilled work migration 42–57
   brain drain debate 53–56
   competition for talent 50–53
   controllability of 57
   denial of visas 32
   discretionary assessment 43–45
   economic impacts 20–23
   employer sponsorship 49–50, **63**
   expression of interest systems 166
   importance of 15
   investor visas 34, 42–43
   low-wage migration compared 58–59
   points systems 44–47
   popularity of 43, 68–69
   sale or auction of work permits 47–49
slave trade 5

INDEX

smuggling 98, 128
social care sector 61, 65, 67, 162
social cohesion 23–31
social integration 23, 27, **28–29**, 31, 62, 83–86
Solomon, Enver 112–113
South Africa 54
South Korea 39, **66**
Spain **12**, **14**, 39, 106
stereotypes 24–27, 44
students 51, 55, 56, 162
Sudan 119
Sunak, Rishi 32
Sweden 39, 111, 124, 159
symbolic policies 41
Syria 120

T

Talent Beyond Boundaries 133
Tanzania 78
Thatcher, Margaret 23
trade negotiations 19, 55
transnational marriages 84–86
Trump, Donald 2, 35, 47
Turkey 55

U

Ugandan Asian refugees 124
Ukrainian refugees 38, **118**, 133, 134
unauthorized migration 91–111
  border enforcement 35, 98
  dangers of **99**, 116, 129
  deportation 33, 102–104, 110, 115, 124
  enforcement abroad 35, 98–99
  ethical issues 31–32
  extent of 101
  human rights applications **108**
  interior enforcement 35, 99–102
  legalization 105–107, 110–111
  offering legal routes 107–110, 132–139
  problematic issues 94–96
  public debates **97**
  reasons for 93–94f
  terminology used **94**
  types of 93
  see also refugees and asylum seekers
undocumented migration *see* unauthorized migration
UNHCR refugee resettlement **121**, 132–133
United Arab Emirates **11**, **14**, 63–64
United Kingdom
  'British way of life' 23
  citizenship test 1, 30–31
  colonial legacy 9, **14**
  Conservative policies 162
  data collection 166
  early border controls 6
  early legislation 5, 6, 44
  Eastern European migrants 25, 26
  family migration 82, 85, 86, 87
  general approach 159
  hostile environment policy 99–101
  human rights applications 107, **108**
  illegal immigration 31–32
  income requirements 82
  investor visas 165
  leaving the EU 2, **12–13**
  Mexican migrants **29**
  Polish community 25
  as popular destination **12**, **13**
  public opinion 3, 37, 37–38, 39, 111

United Kingdom (continued)
- refugees and asylum 38, 124, 126, 128, 129–130, 133, 134–135, 139, 143
- top country of birth **14**
- visa schemes 38, 42–43, 46, 48–49, 61, 77, 78, **164**
- voluntary returns programmes 104
- Windrush scandal 100–101

United States
- caps on green cards **153**
- early immigration 1, 6, 7, 75, 85
- economic influence 68
- family migration 81–82
- Muslim migrants **28–29**
- parent migration 88
- as popular destination **11, 12**
- post-war responsibility 9
- public opinion 37, 39, 110–111, **163–164**
- refugees and asylum **118**, 125, 126, 133, **136–139**, 139, *140*, 142, 143
- southern border 98, 106, *135*, **136–139**, *140*

unauthorized population 101, 106

visa schemes 30, 47–48, 52, 53, 61, 77

V

Venezuela **14**

Vietnam 9

voluntary returns programmes 104

W

wages, impact on 20–21

Windrush scandal 100–101

work migration *see* low-wage work migration; skilled work migration

Y

Yeo, Colin 102

Z

Zimbabwe 54

www.ingramcontent.com/pod-product-compliance
Lightning Source LLC
Chambersburg PA
CBHW031149020426
42333CB00013B/578